The DIY Coaching Manual for Women:

HOW TO TRANSFORM YOUR LIFE IN 12 MONTHS

Dedication

This book is dedicated in loving memory of my mom,
Phyllis Cornell Rozak, who passed away at age 83 on Dec. 29, 2015.
She was my first coach and has always been my biggest supporter.

Thanks, Mom! I owe you, big-time.

Table of Contents

Preface - The "F" word..1

Introduction - Design your own future...........................4

Part 1 Life 6

Chapter 1 - What holds women back..............................7

Chapter 2 - Women and self-esteem...............................9

Chapter 3 - How much are you worth?........................10

Chapter 4 - Clearing obstacles.......................................12

Chapter 5 - How to reinvent yourself...........................13

Chapter 6 - Finding your purpose..................................15

Chapter 7 - Discover what you want.............................16

Chapter 8 - What do you want? Write it down!.........18

Chapter 9 - 3 essential rights...20

Chapter 10 - Coping with failure...................................23

Chapter 11 - Confidence makeover................................25

Chapter 12 - You are in control of you........................27

Chapter 13 - Have faith in yourself...............................28

Chapter 14 - Motivation: Are you an inny or an outy?.....30

Chapter 15 - Finding the value in change....................32

Chapter 16 - Dealing with toxic people.......................34

Chapter 17 - Putting yourself first.................................36

Chapter 18 - How to stop being a doormat.................38

Chapter 19 - How to stop being a bad-luck magnet....41

Chapter 20 - When adult kids mooch...........................43

Chapter 21 - How to stop being the center of the universe.........44

Chapter 22 - Handling criticism.....................................46

Part 2 Career...48

Chapter 23 - Finding your ideal job..............................49

Chapter 24 - Negotiating for what you want...............50

Chapter 25 - You're the boss – act like it....................54

Chapter 26 - Stop micromanaging.................................56

Chapter 27 - When meetings go bad.............................58

Chapter 28 - Leadership..60

Chapter 29 - How to be your own cheerleader...........62

Chapter 30 - Your success mechanism..........................64

Chapter 31 - How fear holds us back............................66

Chapter 32 - Getting SMART...68

Chapter 33 - How to finish what you start...................69

Chapter 34 - Dealing with gossip...................................71

Chapter 35 - Dealing with passive-aggressives...........72

Chapter 36 - Work-life balance.......................................74

Chapter 37 - Sharing the household load.....................76

Chapter 38 - You have the right to your own feelings.....78

Chapter 39 - Releasing your inner control freak........80

Chapter 40 - How to stop doing it all yourself..........81

Chapter 41 - Art of the handshake.................................82

Chapter 42 - Networking for introverts........................84

Chapter 43 - The best way to improve your self-confidence.........86

Chapter 44 - Sexual harassment on the job.................88

Part 3 Health..90

Chapter 45 - Self-esteem and health.............................91

Chapter 46 - Listen to your body...................................93

Chapter 47 - How to stop worrying...............................95

Chapter 48 - Dealing with overwhelm..........................97

Chapter 49 - What to do when life beats you down....98

Chapter 50 - Managing negative emotions..................99

Chapter 51 - Why you get better as you get older......102

Chapter 52 - The year in review.....................................104

Conclusion - Congratulations!..105

Index...106

Special Note

Throughout this book, I reference the workbook. To get the free workbook, please visit the following link:
http://www.key-dynamics.com/diy-coaching-manual-for-women-workbook

If you have any questions, please contact
jackie@key-dynamics.com

THE "F" WORD

"I realize this is probably contrary to your line of work, but what I think is needed is not more coaching for older women, but for society to stop discriminating against them. No matter how well prepared a CV or resume may be, how well-researched an industry, how well prepared for interviews, how updated one's skills may be, there is a measure of job and age discrimination that are very real, and I think that's part of a wider conversation."
Comment from LinkedIn connection

Get society to stop discriminating against older women? Absolutely! "Wider conversation?" Definitely. Here in the United States, we have been having that "wider conversation" since 1869, when women first demanded the right to vote. It took 150 years, but we got there.

The Equal Rights Amendment to the U.S. Constitution was originally penned in 1923. It was put before Congress every year for the next 49 years. It finally was passed in 1972. From there, it went to the individual state legislatures for their ratifications.

From inception to today, with 15 of the 50 states yet to approve of the amendment, 90 years have passed.
90 years!

So... change society? Lovely idea. I'm all for it. At the rate we're going, I'll be long gone before the Equal Rights Amendment is passed. Probably my great-nieces, too.

Back in the 1970s, this entrenched, institutional bias against women made me furious. That's when I adopted the "F" word – feminist, which to many people (including some women, sadly) is just as nasty as the cuss word that begins with the same letter.

The truth will set you free, but first it will piss you off.
Gloria Steinem

Not to me. A feminist advocates for women's rights and seeks political, social and economic equality with men. Try as I might, I can't see the problem with that.

Decades later, when I decided to focus my energies on helping women succeed, that anger resurfaced.

Fortunately, I'd gotten smarter and wiser. I realized I could rail and rant and rave all I wanted, but to what end? It surely hadn't worked 45 years ago; what made me think it was going to work now?

So I put on my coaching hat and said: "Yeah, this is bad. Besides being pissed off, though, what are you going to do about it?"

The solution was clear: Help women, individually and in small groups, improve their lives. That's how to change society... from within.

All I can do is help women of all ages make the best of what they've got – which is often much more than they recognize. Give them the tools to make better choices. Teach them how to ask for more – and get it. Provide tips on how to handle people who treat them like doormats.

Tell them they are better, smarter and stronger than they think they are. Help them stand up for themselves, at home at work and in the marketplace.

A rising tide floats all boats. When women are stronger, when they make the money they deserve, when they speak up, they not only make life better for themselves, they improve society as a whole.
Coaching women is what gives me joy. It gets me out of bed in the morning. But I won't lie to you – sometimes, it's incredibly sad, too.

Women have been so conditioned to give instead of ask, stay silent instead of speak up, seek levels of perfection that simply do not exist, nurture guilt instead of personal pride that many feel they don't have any choices.

That's a lie. It's a story they've been told so many times that they believe it themselves.

They don't believe they deserve better, but they do.

By the time women seek my help, a very few of them are so beaten down that they have lost all – and I do mean all – sense of balance and proportion. Everything is a catastrophe, from getting stuck in traffic to being fired from their 30-year job. They often have no idea what is right and what is wrong for themselves and they take on the protective coloration of the expectations of others.

And they are miserable.

Some wonder why they are the way they are, how they got to this place. My answer: Ultimately, it doesn't matter. If they can't get beyond that, I suggest therapy.

What's important now is if they can move on from the "why" to "what can I do going forward."

If they can move forward, then we've got the start of a plan that will bring real changes to their lives and the opportunity for real happiness – which always starts on the inside.

So this isn't just my business. It's my passion. That's why I'm a success coach for women: I focus on where I can do the most good and make the largest contribution to achieving those ideals I hold dear.
The challenge of working with women who have bottomed-out is where to begin. And the answer to that is the same as to the "why" question: It doesn't matter.

Start anywhere.

I have a strong sense of self, I am confident, I have mad skills gained from nearly 40 years as a newspaper executive and later as the CEO of a nonprofit. And it still took me 3 years of trial and error, mostly learning what I didn't want, before I "came home" to what I was meant to do.

The sooner you begin – anywhere – the sooner you'll end up where you want to be; the sooner you will find your strength and your power. When you're in that sweet spot, those around you begin to change as well.

And because of your individual strength, multiplied by hundreds and thousands, society changes, too.

START ANYWHERE. JUST BEGIN.

Jackie Harder
JANUARY 2016

INTRODUCTION
DESIGN YOUR OWN FUTURE

You are stronger, smarter and better than you think you are.

How could I possibly know that? Because virtually every woman I have met is convinced, on some level, that she is not worthy, not deserving, not able or capable – somehow "less than" everyone else.

Many even feel they are imposters, faking it in a world of perfect people and convinced that at any moment, they will be unmasked for the "less than" person that they are.

It's simply not true. And my goal, in this book, is to help you come to that realization. To understand and accept the phenomenal, powerful woman you truly are.

This book is not about feeding you a bunch of motivation or inspirational quotes, patting you on the shoulder and saying: "OK – now go get 'em, girl!"

Sure, you'll find plenty of motivation and inspiration here (I sincerely hope!), but more than that, you'll find concrete, actionable steps to help guide you to where you want to be. Not sure where that is? Not sure, even, who you are? No clue of your goals, passions or strengths?
Gotcha covered.

I've got exercises – called Coaching Requests – that will help you uncover your passion, find your life's purpose, teach you how to stand up for yourself and get what you want out of life. You'll also find information about how to determine what you're worth, how to handle dicey work situations, how to deal with toxic people and gossips, how to create your own success mechanism and how to make time for what's important.

And more. Much more.

In fact, I had trouble limiting myself in this book. I have been writing about these topics and coaching women – just like you – since 2003. Officially, that is; that's when I got my coaching credentials.

But long before that – during my entire 30-year career as a newspaper executive – I've been coaching people to help them find their own path and their own solutions. I've been giving them the tools they need to excel not just at work but in life as well.

Coaching is about the whole person, not just bits and pieces scattered around the landscape. We cannot separate what we do from who we are. This is especially true these days as the lines between work and life are increasingly blurred thanks (or no thanks) to the Internet, cell phones and instant communication channels.

What affects us in one area of our lives impacts all other areas.

So you'll find information and techniques here about how to negotiate for a raise, how to handle stress, how to share the household workload and everything in between.

You'll see lots of "how to's" in this book and that's deliberate. Insight is great; my goal is to help you take those insights and do something about them.

I've designed this manual to be as close to one-on-one coaching as possible. I've broken it into 52 chapters – one for each week of the year, just as if you and I were talking each week on a coaching call.

At the end of each chapter, you will find the Coaching Requests. They are just like homework, but without the teacher standing over your shoulder, demanding why it's not done!

Coaching is self-motivated; you've got to do the work to see the results. I can give you the tools; I can't make you do the work. That's all on you.

I have organized the book's content in broad strokes. The first part is about personal development and is designed to give you a strong foundation. The middle part covers some of the most pressing workplace issues. And, the last part focuses on some vexing concerns that sometimes damage our mental and emotional health.

Feel free to skip around. Each chapter is intended to stand alone. As you go through the book, you will see a number of themes repeated. That's deliberate, too; sometimes it takes a lot of repetition for concepts to sink in! Sometimes you need to hear it 500 times before you get it at No. 501.

Coaching is the most gratifying work you'll do – because in the end, you, too, will learn how much stronger, smarter and better you really are.

Happy new you!

Part 1 LIFE

CHAPTER 1
WHAT HOLDS WOMEN BACK

Why don't more women achieve greater success? By and large, it's all in their head.

Yes, I understand that there are still too many institutionalized barriers that prevent women from reaching the levels of success they deserve. I also know, from the hundreds of women I interact with every day, that most of what keeps women in a "less than" position is how they perceive themselves.

- » "I'd love to go for that job, but *I don't know enough.*"
- » *"I'm not sure* I could lead a team."
- » "That job is huge – it's *too much of a stretch for me.*"
- » *"Where could I get the help* I need to do that?"
- » "I have only about 80% of the skills I need for that position. That's *not good enough.*"
- » *"I'm not ready* to take on that big a challenge."
- » *"I don't think* I have the experience I need to do that."

There are two themes here: our belief that we need to be perfect and our belief that we're not good enough, smart enough or strong enough to figure out how to overcome our challenges.

This is in stark contrast to men, who are comfortable with having about 60% of what they need to do the job before they go for it. Their attitude: "Hey – good enough!" And it usually is, because they are confident that they can grow into the job.

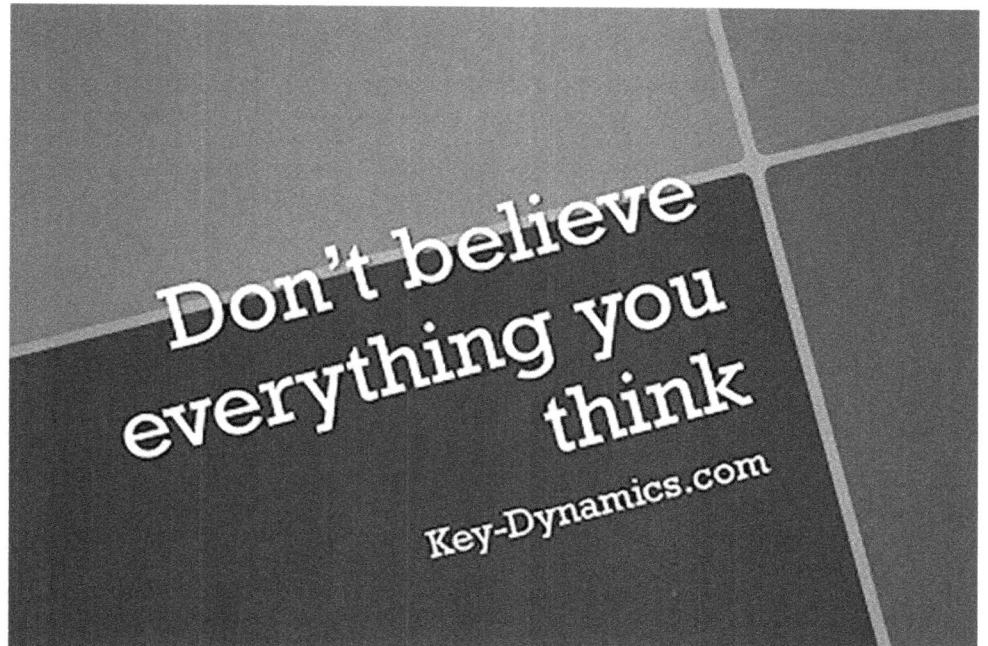

Don't believe everything you think

Key-Dynamics.com

We women also have a tendency to want a guaranteed outcome, and if that outcome doesn't materialize, it makes us feel like we have failed. We are governed by our egos – or lack thereof – and that's another thing that holds us back.

The ironic thing about that is that many of us leap into motherhood not knowing if we'll be a good parent. First-time moms have zero experience with the responsibilities of 24/7 childcare. They take on a "job" that will last a minimum of 18 years – and in actuality, a job that lasts for their lifetime – with few skills in child psychology and development.

This is the biggest challenge of their lives... and they still do it, despite a lack of experience, skills and assistance.

And there is certainly no guarantee of the outcome.

When you think about it, the opportunities for failure at parenthood are much more numerous and the consequences much graver. What's the worst that can happen when you take on a new job and fail? You lose the job?

Everyone gets fired. Everyone. Smart, self-confident women use that "failure" as a learning experience to move far beyond their perceived limits.

YOU are your greatest resource – your intelligence, your determination and your belief in yourself. Sure, skills are important, but they are a remarkably small part of your overall success and they can be learned.

Here are some concrete steps you can take to stop holding yourself back.

COACHING REQUEST

What challenge would you like to address? What dream do you want to follow? Pick something that speaks to you and complete the following.

» **ASSESS THE RISK.** Figure out what is the worst that can happen and then assign a percentage to it. The worst that can happen: I'll lose the job. The probability that that will happen: 20%.

» **HOW CAN YOU MINIMIZE THE RISK?** What resources can you call on to help you keep the risk to a manageable level? Who – or what – can you turn to for help?

» **START!** Your heart is pounding, your mouth is dry and your palms are wet. So what? None of these will kill you. The very worst part about doing something that challenges you is taking that first step. But once you've done that and discover that you have not burst into flames, the next step will be easier – and will get progressively easier as you go. I promise!

» **EVALUATE.** Was it worth it? Would you do it again? What would you do differently? I'm not a big believer in failure, because I think every tumble and wrong turn is a learning experience that can be used for the next adventure. The more you do, the more you learn.

CHAPTER 2
WOMEN AND SELF-ESTEEM

DOES THIS SOUND LIKE SOMEONE YOU KNOW?

» A woman I know was recently named among the top 25 influencers in her niche in the fourth largest city in America. She asked, "Is this something I should add to my stuff?"

» Another was quoted extensively on topics within her area of expertise, in major publications online and in print... and she downplays it.

» A third was named the hero of her company, one of the largest in the United States. Why? She refused to talk about it.

Forget about "Does this sound like someone you know?" Does this sound like you?

Women have a hard time taking deserved credit, partially because we have been taught that it's unfeminine to stand front and center, to call attention to themselves. We believe that people will think less of us if we point out the great things that we have achieved through our own hard work, talent and skill.

Time to get over that. Way past time.

If you suffer from unwarranted bashfulness or reluctance to take credit where credit is due, this Coaching Request is for you.

COACHING REQUEST

Where do you want to step up your game? Pick an area of your life, or even a specific situation, where you'd like to gain more personal power.

» **FIGURE OUT WHY YOU FEEL THE WAY YOU DO.** Pick a quiet location where you will be undisturbed for about 30 minutes. Close your eyes and travel to a time in your life when you felt strong and confident. Re-experience that with all your senses. Then ask yourself: "Why do I feel ___?"

» **PAY ATTENTION TO THE FIRST ANSWER YOU GET.** It's coming from your heart. The second answer that comes up will be your brain arguing against the first answer; ignore it.

» **LISTEN TO YOUR SELF-TALK.** What are you telling yourself about the situation? What are you telling yourself about your own role in it? You may be parroting something you heard as a child and have never reexamined. You're now an adult. You can make your own choices.

» **ARE YOU INDULGING IN "ALL OR NOTHING" THINKING?** Are you screening out the positive and focusing only on the negative? Are you jumping to negative conclusions? Are you confusing feelings with facts? You may feel like you don't have much going for you, but is that actually true? Ask people you trust to give you the straight skinny. I think you'll be amazed.

CHAPTER 3
HOW MUCH ARE YOU WORTH?

"I CAN'T AFFORD IT."

How many times have you said this, to sales people, family members or to yourself?

Many times, it makes sense. I can't afford a Bentley Continental GT convertible. Nor am I in the market for an expensive home on Miami Beach. Although a girl can certainly dream!

But there are absolutely two things I can and must invest in – me and my business.

I learned very early on, when I devoted myself full time to build my business, Key Dynamics Coaching and Consulting. that I would have to look beyond my local market if I wanted to succeed. That required a strategic investment in my business – social media training and a comprehensive inbound marketing component.

Could I afford it? My bank balance squealed, "No!" I would have to dip into my retirement savings in order to make these investments. As a woman who loves security, that gave me the heebie-jeebies.

But I knew that's what they were – investments – in me and in my business. So I gritted my teeth and wrote the checks

They turned out to be wise choices. Since taking my social media training, I have built a solid, online presence on three platforms. My website visits have gone into the stratosphere.

Am I where I want to be? Have I achieved intergalactic domination yet? No. But I am a lot closer than when I started – and that's because I decided to make two crucial investments that I initially told myself I couldn't afford.

I see the same tendency in women who say, in knee-jerk fashion, that they cannot afford to make an investment in themselves. Sadly, they don't feel they deserve it.

They believe they can't afford to learn new skills that would allow them to become stronger, more self-sufficient, more self-confident, more "worthy" to themselves and others. To these women, I say: How much are you worth... to yourself?

There is more to that answer, of course, than what you see on a bank statement.

There is the sense of worth that comes from knowing you have intrinsic value as a human being who has much to offer the world. If you stepped back and took stock of all the things you've done, all the things you've learned, you would be amazed at the value you do have. (You'll get a chance to compile such a list in this book.)

The "I can't afford it" mindset is self-limiting. If you don't value who you are now, you will never get more of

Our biggest limitations are what we believe about ourselves

what you want, because you don't think you deserve it.

If you are not confident in yourself, your abilities and your skills, there is no way you are going to be able to negotiate a higher salary. There is no way that you'll be able to get a better job. There is no way you're going to be able to stop people from pushing you around, taking advantage of you and getting you to do what they want you to do, as opposed to what is good and right for you.

The same women who say they can't afford to invest in themselves still manage to buy a skinny latte every day on their way to work. They can find the money for a $20 lunch a couple times a month or splurge on dinner at a fancy restaurant.

It's not so much a lack of funds as it is a lack of belief in themselves, that they are worth it. Until they learn that, they will never reach the level of success they want – and that they are more than capable of achieving.

The following Coaching Request is designed to help you determine your baseline beliefs in yourself. If you can answer all these questions in the affirmative, you've got a good foundation. If, on the other hand, you answer "no" more than "yes," you've got some work to do!

COACHING REQUEST

» I focus on what's possible.
» I deserve the best.
» I appreciate everything I have.
» I can learn this.
» I have a plan to get to where I want to be.
» I have everything I want.
» I'm worth it.
» I look at challenges as opportunities.
» I'm OK with making mistakes.
» When something goes wrong, I ask myself, "What can I create from this?"

CHAPTER 4
CLEARING OBSTACLES

What do you do when you find your way is unexpectedly blocked?

You can roll over on your back, exposing your belly in submission to the alpha dog that is challenging you. Or you embrace your challenges and make them work for you instead of against you.

Understand that there is opportunity hidden in every challenge. It just takes a different mindset, a different way of framing your experience, and looking at it from a positive point of view rather than seeing it through the eyes of a victim.

Here's an example from one of my clients: She was having issues at work, being criticized and blocked at every turn by her new boss. Despite stellar reviews for more than 10 years, he found a way to get rid of her – he abolished her job altogether.

After the shock and feeling of devastation wore off (and I recommend you embrace those feelings so you can move past them), we talked about what she wanted to do with her life. She decided that she wanted to continue what she'd been doing, what she's passionate about, but in her own business.

Six months later, she is thriving. She's got plenty of clients and is expanding her services. Today, she looks back at what was the most shattering professional experience of her life – and is grateful that it propelled her forward. She's happier than she's ever been.

You are just like her. You have an incredible array of life experiences, common sense and intuition to help you embrace your challenges. Give yourself permission to unleash your creativity, and be confident enough to recognize your own inner wisdom.

COACHING REQUEST

>> *IDENTIFY ONE THING THAT'S HOLDING YOU BACK AND REFRAME IT.* This exercise is adapted from the Freeze-Frame technique found in *The HeartMath Solution* by Doc Childre and Howard Martin.

- Set aside about 30 minutes.
- Find a comfortable spot, away from any kind of intrusion.
- Think back to a place and time when you were happy, relaxed, loved, stress-free and so on.
- Re-experience as much about that place and time as you can, until you feel you are there once again.
- Ask your heart: "How can I turn this 'negative' into something positive?"
- Listen to the answer. And don't let your brain try to talk you out of it!

CHAPTER 5

HOW TO REINVENT YOURSELF

First it's one small thing and then another and you don't really pay attention because... well... life is like that – full of ups and downs. But one day you wake up and say: "Wait! Something just ain't right here."

If you have that squirmy, floaty feeling in your belly and wonder what the heck's going on, check out this list to figure out if it's time to change your life.

DO YOU:

>> **DREAD GOING TO WORK?** We all have those days when the idea of going to work is as attractive as a root canal without the Novocain. But when it's every day – or even more days that not, that's a significant clue.

>> **LIVE IN THE PAST?** One of the saddest things is hearing someone say, "High school was the best time of my life." If you are stuck in the past – an old relationship, a former job, your college years, whatever – and it takes away from your enjoyment of today, it's time to reassess.

> When the **pain of where you are** is greater than the **fear of the unknown,**
>
> ## that's when you'll change
>
> EMPOWERING WOMEN | KEY-DYNAMICS.COM

>> **DREAM ENDLESSLY ABOUT THE FUTURE?** Dreaming about the future is great. It can be a great motivator to do new things. However, when that's all you think about, it can take away from your here and now... and doing what needs to be done to make those dreams come true.

>> **NEED TO TAKE A PILL?** Everyone tells you to chill out. Or they start to avoid you because you complain all the time.

>> **ENVY OTHER PEOPLE THEIR SUCCESS?** We all feel a bit of envy when someone – especially someone you know personally – makes it big and you're still struggling. What I'm talking about here is more obsessive than that, until it blackens your mood all the time and makes you resentful.

>> **WAKE UP TIRED?** Again, this is something that we all experience on occasion, but when it happens day in and day out, something is wrong. It generally means we're not taking good care of ourselves, including bad eating habits, lack of exercise, working too much and ignoring our own needs.

>> **SLEEP POORLY?** You either wake up a lot during the night, can't get to sleep, get up well before you are rested or go to bed early and sleep for 10 to 12 hours.

>> **HAVE ANTS IN YOUR PANTS?** You're restless. You can't stay focused. You've got lots of nervous energy and nowhere to blow it off. You need to be doing, doing, doing all the time but in many cases, you have no idea what it is you need to be doing. You just know that "it" – what you're doing right now – isn't really "it" at all.

>> **GET ANNOYED ALL THE TIME?** Traffic is too fast or too slow. The AC is too hot or too cold. The guy in the next cubby talks too much or is too lazy. Your work is too hard or too boring. Your kids, your spouse, your job, the grocery store, the gas pump – everything annoys you.

» **FEEL LIKE YOU'RE WAITING FOR THE OTHER SHOE TO DROP?** You're anxious, because you know something bad is about to happen. You don't know what it is, but you know it's there. And it's coming for you.

» **NOT CARE ABOUT ANYTHING?** Nothing is important – not brushing your hair or taking a shower or showing up at the parent-teacher conference or getting the report finished on time or checking your email. It's all just too much.

» **WONDER "IS THIS ALL THERE IS?"** Your whole life is crap, from the minute you wake up until you hit the sack. You think there's got to be something more in life than what you're doing.

If many of these have your name written all over of them, this is your wake-up call. Something has to give. Don't let it be your sanity.

COACHING REQUEST

» **MAKE AN APPOINTMENT WITH YOUR DOCTOR** to make sure there's nothing physically wrong with you.

» **IF YOU CHECK OUT PHYSICALLY,** you may need a good therapist to help you scale those walls you just can't climb by yourself. Ask your doctor for some names; ask friends to see if they know of anyone good. If the first one isn't a good match, keep looking. Asking for help when you need it is a sign of strength, not weakness.

» **IF EVERYTHING ELSE IS A GO, CONSIDER COACHING.** Coaching helps you figure out your path forward and provides support and accountability so you can make the changes you want in your life. Do your research, see who you think would be a good fit and set up a consultation. Most coaches will offer one for free.

CHAPTER 6
FINDING YOUR PURPOSE

Life is so busy, so full of distractions, with so many items on our to-do lists that our lives sometimes get out of focus. We are adrift and many times we don't even know it because we're always on the move... somewhere. Even if that destination isn't really where we want to go.

What's missing, in many cases, is a feeling of purpose. If that resonates with you, go through the following Coaching Request to help you discover your life purpose.

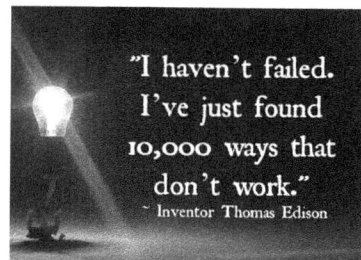

> "I haven't failed. I've just found 10,000 ways that don't work."
> ~ Inventor Thomas Edison

COACHING REQUEST

» **WHAT MAKES YOU FEEL ALIVE?** Close your eyes in a quiet location and ask yourself that question. What gives you energy? What gets your blood moving, brightens your day?

» **WHAT ACCOMPLISHMENTS ARE YOU MOST PROUD OF?** Is it raising a family? Having a successful business? Climbing mountains? Mentoring others?

» **WHAT WOULD YOU LIKE PEOPLE TO SAY ABOUT YOU DURING YOUR EULOGY?** Kind, generous, helpful, funny, smart, loving, frugal, hard-working, bold? Make your list as long as you can and then ask yourself: Am I that person today? If not, what do I need to change?

» **WHO DO YOU ADMIRE MOST AND WHY?** Is it Oprah Winfrey, for her amazing rags-to-riches story? Is it Stephen Hawking, the theoretical physicist who has achieved greatness despite his debilitating Lou Gehrig's disease? Maybe it's Thomas Edison, the man who failed 10,000 times before he found the solution to a workable light bulb. Note as many people as you wish and don't forget to include why.

» **IF THERE IS ONE GLOBAL PROBLEM YOU COULD SOLVE, WHAT WOULD IT BE?** If you have ideas on solutions, that's great! Anyone can (and does) criticize; how to fix it is what's important. If you can't come up with a solution, that's OK, too. But imagine what the final result would look like if you solved the problem.

» **WHAT'S THE VISION OF YOUR LIFE?** Look at all your answers thus far for clues. What are the common threads that give color to your life?

» **WHAT ARE YOU DOING NOW THAT'S KEEPING YOU FROM PUTTING THAT VISION OR PURPOSE INTO ACTION?** List as many of these stumbling blocks as you can.

» **WHAT ARE THE COMMONALITIES?** Based on the information you've gathered, what are the common threads? And even more important, what are the contradictions? Understand there is no right or wrong answer; this is your life and you get to choose how to live it. Don't let anyone tell you differently.

» **WRITE DOWN THREE POSSIBLE LIFE PURPOSES.** How do they feel to you? Does one resonate more strongly than the others?

For more information, be sure to check out the accompanying workbook.

CHAPTER 7

DISCOVER WHAT YOU WANT

WHAT DO YOU WANT?

Many women don't have a clue – like the highly paid, and recently laid-off professional who came to me, looking to answer just that question.

She had spent half her life in her now-former profession, not because she really liked it, but because the money was great.

And now here she was: No job, no idea where to go – and possibly most unnerving of all – no feeling of passion, no notion of what gets her motor running.

It's a sad but fairly common occurrence, especially for those of us who are in our 40s and 50s, who take a long look at their lives and wonder, "Is this it? Am I where I want to be?"

WHAT DO YOU WANT?

Women will either rattle off a memorized, meaningless litany of things they are supposed to want – like a million dollars, a big house on the water, an attractive mate, a well-paying job – without even thinking about it. Or, conversely, they get that stricken, half-guilty look that says, "Am I allowed to want things for myself?"

THAT LAST QUESTION IS THE EASIEST OF ALL TO ANSWER.

Yes, you ARE allowed to want things for yourself. In fact, it's required. And the more passionate you are about the things you want, the more likely you are to get them.

We often get disconnected from our passion by well-meaning people who say they want the best for us, but who may instead be motivated (innocently and otherwise) by what's best for them.

Your passion of becoming a world-renown chef, for instance, could be derailed by loved ones, who don't want you to go off to culinary school and leave them behind.

Your desire to invent marvelous new things could be discounted by people who fear they would lose status or income should you quit your job to purse your dream.

Where it gets tricky is figuring out what, exactly, it is that you want. The following exercise will make it easier.

COACHING REQUEST

>> **MAKE A LIST, STREAM OF CONSCIOUSNESS, OF WHAT YOU WANT.** Don't think about it and don't worry

It's OK to want things for yourself

Empowering Women | Key Dynamics

about putting it in any particular order. Just write down everything you want. Be as wild and crazy as you like. Don't scratch off anything.

» **WHEN YOUR LIST IS FINISHED**, ask yourself these questions, and connect with your heart and your gut to get the answers:

- ○ Did your "wants" flow from your fingertips pretty much in the order of importance to you?
- ○ Are any of these "wants" actually "shoulds," either imposed by others or by some internal censor that passes judgment on what is "right" for you to want?
- ○ Do you see a pattern? If so, how does it make you feel? For example, if your wants lean toward amassing wealth, is it really the money you want – or the feeling of security you get from having cash in the bank? If you see lots of social activities on your list, is it really the "doing" that you want in your life, or is it the feeling of connection you get from being with other people?

» **WHAT LOOKS NUTTY**, out of the question, absurd, ridiculous and so on? These are often those things that fuel our passions. Don't discount them!

CHAPTER 8
WHAT DO YOU WANT? WRITE IT DOWN!

I love lists, as you will discover. There is something... magical... about them.

Pragmatically, lists help smooth the path of everyday life. Jot down what you want/need to do every day, prioritize it, and if you stick with it, not only will you get more done (on average, 30% for me) but it will be stuff worth getting done.

But the magic goes far beyond the practical.

I recall the day, several years ago, when I sat down with my planner and quickly jotted down five goals I wanted to achieve that year. And then promptly ignored it (color me blushing). Imagine my delight – and shock and surprise – when, repeating the exercise a year later, I discovered that I had accomplished three of the major goals I wanted to reach.

Without even trying.

As amazing as that is, it is hardly news.

More than 60 years ago, researchers studied a group of 100 Harvard Business School graduates. Among other things, they all wanted to be rich. During a follow-up 10 years later, the researchers learned that 90% of the wealth was concentrated in the hands of 10% of grads. Why?

The significant difference between the two groups was that the rich grads had **WRITTEN DOWN THEIR GOALS.**

It worked for those Harvard boys. It worked for me. There's no reason why it shouldn't work for you, too.

Here's how to get started.

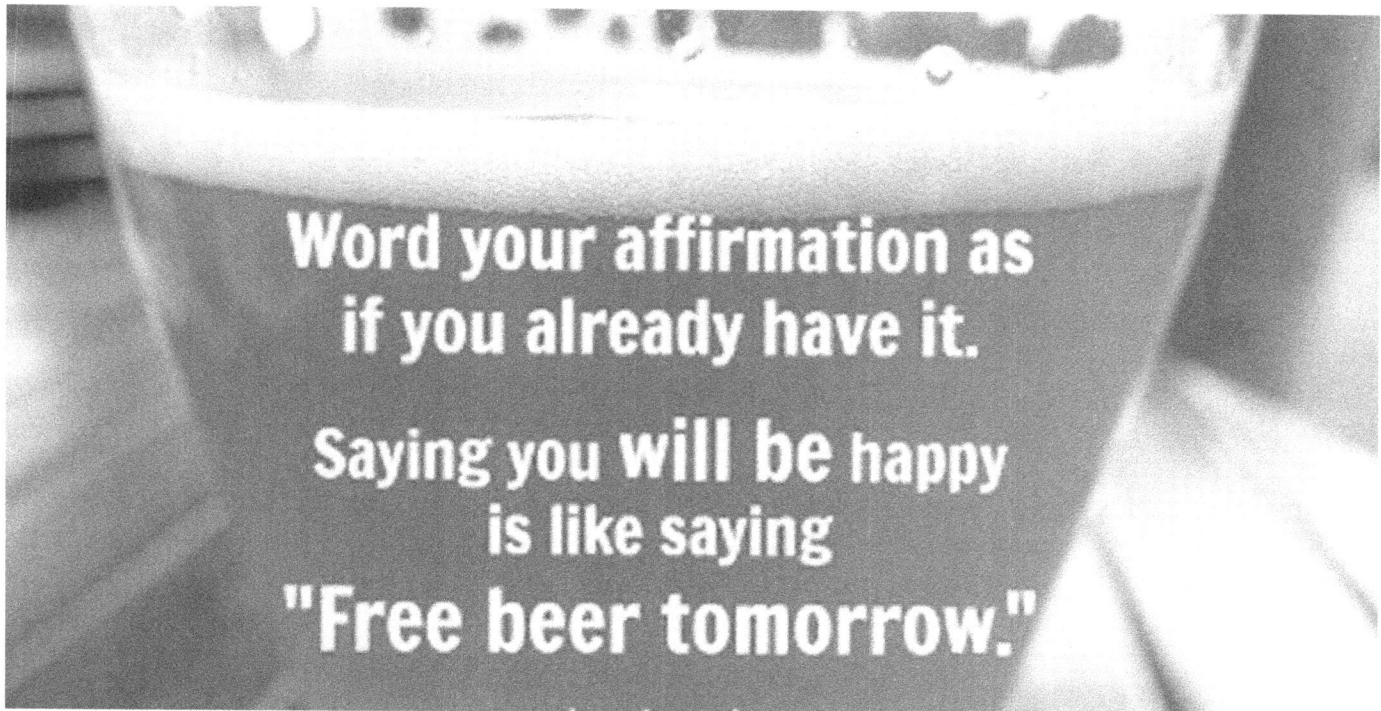

Word your affirmation as if you already have it.

Saying you **will be** happy is like saying **"Free beer tomorrow."**

COACHING REQUEST

» *USE PEN (OR EVEN PENCIL) AND PAPER TO MAKE YOUR GOALS LIST.* Yes, it's slower than using the computer. That's the point. Writing things down helps install these goals in your gray matter. And using a pencil is better; that infinitesimal extra drag of lead over paper has been shown to be even more effective.

» *DON'T WORRY (RIGHT NOW) ABOUT WHICH IS MOST IMPORTANT.* Just get it all down.

» *BE SURE YOUR VERBS ARE ACTIVE AND PRESENT TENSE.* You want to give your brain the notion of action. By writing that you have already achieved what you want by using present-tense verbs, you are reinforcing your goals. Your brain does not know the difference between what you have and what you want. It just helps you get it.

» *BANISH NEGATIVE WORDS.* Negative words are not just "never" and "don't." It's what you pair with them. For example, "don't be rude" emphasizes "rude," while "be nice" clearly states what you want.

» *REPLACE THE IMPRECISE WITH SPECIFICS.* "Make more money" isn't nearly as precise or effective as "earn at least $200,000 a year."

» *READ YOUR LIST EVERY MORNING.* This reminds your brain what's important and where you're going.

» *REFINE YOUR PHRASING.* You may notice that you have used different language for the same goals; those are the most important to you. Focus on them.

» *REWRITE YOUR LIST EVERY SO OFTEN.* It helps keep them on the top of your mind.

» *PAY ATTENTION.* You will start to see forward movement on your list almost immediately. That's because you will begin to make choices – some of them subconsciously – that take you closer to your goals. Also, by reminding yourself daily of what you want, you are more apt to recognize the opportunities that will help you get there.

CHAPTER 9
3 ESSENTIAL RIGHTS

How would your life change if you used these two sentences?

I WANT/LIKE _____.
I DON'T WANT/LIKE _____.

Many women don't think they have the right to want (or not want) things for themselves. Wanting things for ourselves, we are told, makes us appear greedy or needy or pushy or unladylike. We have been taught to put the needs of others before our own, particularly in our personal lives.

The thing is, we ask for what we want all the time – and don't think a thing about it.

» You go to the grocery store and you tell the man behind the deli counter, "I want an Italian sub without mayo."
» You go to the hair stylist and say, "I like the curly look but I don't want to get a perm."
» You go to the library and tell the librarian, "I want a great book and I don't like to read anything socially significant."
» Your kids have just torn up your house. "I want this mess cleaned up in 10 minutes," you say, "and I don't want to hear any backtalk."

A **BOLD** coaching request

Fill in the blanks:

• I want _____.

• I don't want _____.

Key-Dynamics.com

Easy-peasy, right? Admittedly, there's not much at stake in these conversations, but the same skills you already have can be applied to dicier situations. And they work. You need a new car. You tell the salesman, "I want a four-door sedan and I don't want to spend more than $10,000."

You're not getting the attention you want from a loved one. "I want to spend more time with you," you say, "and I don't want to be interrupted by kids or cell phones."

Here are three essential rights, outlined by Dr. Manuel J. Smith in his highly recommended book, *When I Say No, I Feel Guilty*.

You have the right to want what you want, and don't want, and to tell people in your life about it.

It's not a matter of being right or wrong. It's about being true to who you are, and owning your own wishes and desires. It's about what works for you and what doesn't. **IT DOESN'T HAVE TO BE FAIR, LOGICAL OR ANYTHING ELSE.** It's you and your life, and you owe it to yourself, and others, to be honest about it.

You have the right to offer no reasons or excuses for justifying your behavior.

By giving people the right to question your decisions, you are living by their rules and abiding by their judgment that you are "wrong" for your decision. When you explain your behavior, you are tacitly agreeing that they have the right to determine what you do. And when you do it and to whom and for how long.

Is that what you want – to be governed by what other people think is right for you?

You have the right to decide if you are responsible for finding solutions to other people's problems.

It's a pretty common thought process, especially for us women: We believe we have an obligation to sacrifice what we want to keep relationships, other people and institutions from falling apart. Taking that another step further, that means if we have problems with this, then we need to change, not vice versa.

I say bullshit.

Going back to the car example: If the vehicle you buy is a lemon, do you not have the right to get your money back or a replacement – even if it means the dealer or the manufacturer takes a hit?

If the counterman gives you mayo on your sub when you specifically requested no mayo, do you not have the right to get a new one, even if it means throwing the other one away?

It's all about setting boundaries, and then sticking to them – without guilt.

Setting boundaries is not about blame. It's telling the other person honestly how you feel about their behavior and letting them know how you want to be treated.

You have two choices in most situations: You can give in (and hate yourself) or speak up and feel strong and empowered.

Fortunately, there are ways to have these types of conversations that allow you to speak your mind – what you want and don't want.

Here's how to do the latter.

COACHING REQUEST

» **PICK A SPECIFIC EXAMPLE OF THE BEHAVIOR YOU'D LIKE THEM TO STOP.**

» **CHOOSE A TIME AND PLACE TO HAVE THE CONVERSATION.** If possible, don't react in the heat of the moment when your emotions are running high.

» **CLEARLY DESCRIBE THE BEHAVIOR YOU'D LIKE TO CHANGE WITHOUT BLAMING,** using an "I" statement: "I don't like it when you try to pass along your work to me and I want you to stop." Or "I feel disrespected when you say XX to me."

» **KEEP YOUR LANGUAGE NEUTRAL AND NON-BLAMING.** This is not an argument. You have the right to express yourself and you don't have to justify what you're feeling or saying.

» **STICK TO YOUR MAIN POINT.** You want the behavior to stop. Don't get sidetracked.

» **GET THEIR AGREEMENT.** This is a key step! By getting their agreement to stop, you'll have the ammo you need later to get them back on the wagon when they fall off. And they generally will.

» **EXPECT PUSHBACK.** Some people will agree right way, because they honestly had no idea how their behavior was impacting you. Others, however, will dance all around the topic. The most manipulative will push it back on you, telling you that you're too sensitive, you don't love them anymore or that it's for your own good, etc.

» **TRY THE "BROKEN RECORD" TECHNIQUE.** This is a great way to answer the manipulator without becoming emotional or getting into an argument. Say something like, "I know you may think I'm being too sensitive, but it really bothers me when you pass your work on to me, and I'd like you to stop. Will you agree to stop?" Note: You are not saying the other person is right. You are just acknowledging what he said, and still sticking to your main point.

» **REPEAT.** You may have to repeat this step many times to get the point across. Don't give up and don't give in!

» **WHEN THE BEHAVIOR HAPPENS AGAIN,** remind them of their agreement and ask them to stop the behavior immediately.

» **WHEN YOU'VE HAD ENOUGH,** say: "You're trying to dump your work on me again. I've asked you not to do this and you agreed you would stop. If you do it again, I'm going to _____." In a workplace situation. it could be talking to the boss or complaining to HR. At home, it could be taking away privileges.

» **PULL THE TRIGGER ON THE CONSEQUENCES IF THE BEHAVIOR PERSISTS.**

CHAPTER 10
COPING WITH FAILURE

Aren't we all our own worst critics? Don't we have high expectations for ourselves and harshly judge ourselves as "unworthy" when we fail?

There is no such thing as "failure." Consider it, instead, a "course correction."

You make a left instead of a right. Have you "failed?" Do you grimly keep heading in that direction even when you know you need to turn around? Or do you throw up your hands, declare, "It's no use! I'll never get to that place" and just sit there?

Of course not! You learned from what didn't work, made the necessary changes and kept moving.

> How you deal with failure is a measure of success
>
> { Key-Dynamics.com

Completing the following Coaching Request will help get you back on your path.

COACHING REQUEST

» **WHAT DID YOU DO WRONG?** Where did you get off course? Write it down, if you know; ask for feedback if you don't.

» **WHAT YOU CAN DO DIFFERENTLY?** There is always more than one road to the goal.

» **OPEN YOURSELF TO THE POSSIBILITIES.** Maybe your failure – especially if it's just one more piece of a larger pattern – is your subconscious' signal that you weren't meant to go in that direction after all. I once coached a woman who, in her first call, said she wanted to get back into big business. By the second call, she had thought more about her choices and decided she wanted to open a B&B instead.

» **BEGIN.** What's your first move? Even the smallest step is a step forward. Trying to bite off too big a chunk is what chokes us. Start with your big task – your goal – and break it down into the smallest pieces possible. Begin.

» **KEEP MOVING.** Maybe your hardships are a bit bigger than gaining a pound instead of losing one. Maybe you're going through the loss of a loved one, a job, a home. Here's the good news: You will get through it. As awful and overwhelming as it seems now, nothing lasts forever. What steps can you take to help you move through it? Who can help? Pick a sympathetic and objective person (your pastor, a coach, a therapist) who wants what's best for you. Watch out for people who have skin in your game. Hang in there!

» **REVIEW.** Yes, you CAN do this. Whatever it is, you can do it. There is no problem so large it can't be solved. Make a list every night before you go to bed. What good things happened to you during the day? What did you accomplish? What positive things are in your life? Start your list with "I woke up this morning." Take it from there.

» **FRAME YOUR THINKING POSITIVELY.** Instead of "I didn't kill my boss today," say, "I had pleasant conversations with my boss." Instead of "I didn't yell at my kids," say, "I treated my kids with a cool head." This reinforces what's right instead of focusing on what's not. This perspective allows you to build momentum. By creating and reviewing your list before you go to bed, you'll find it easier to go to sleep and wake up rested... knowing that yes, you can do this.

CHAPTER 11
CONFIDENCE MAKEOVER

Feeling down in the dumps? Beating yourself up for not looking like a super-model? Can't find the right job – or any job – or clients are thin on the ground? You're probably overdue for a confidence makeover.

Here are some tips that will help you do just that. Use them, practice them and keep moving ahead!

COACHING REQUEST

» **LEARN HOW TO BE AN EFFECTIVE PUBLIC SPEAKER.** This is always my A-No. 1 tip for building self-confidence. I cannot emphasize enough how much confidence you will gain, in every area of your life, once you can speak to a group of people. The good news: It's a learned skill, and the more you practice, the better you'll get. Find a Toastmasters or other public-speaking group in your area and sign up. It will be the absolute best investment of your time — and yourself — that you can make.

Public speaking is the best way to build
self-confidence

» **DRESS FOR IT.** Back in my newspaper days, I knew there would be times when all hell would break loose. Those were the days I went into my closet and pulled out my "armor" — my favorite red dress. It was well-made, nicely tailored and made me feel like a million bucks. And guess what? When I was wearing my red dress, no one EVER gave me grief. The dress made me psychologically bulletproof, and other people sensed it. If you don't have your own version of a red dress in your closet, go get one. Spend whatever you need to in order to KNOW you look fabulous... and powerful. It works.

» **DUMP THE NEGATIVE NELLIES.** If you've got people around you who are chomping away at your self-confidence, get rid of them. Bless them and release them from your life, if you can. If you can't, limit your exposure to them.

» **FEED YOUR BRAIN.** What would you like to learn? Quantum physics? How to take great photographs, graft plants, tune your engine... anything at all? Spend some time doing that. If it's not related directly to your job or your business, give yourself bonus points. Being a well-rounded human being is another way to feel better about yourself.

» **GET OFF YOUR BUTT.** Physical activity of any kind will not only improve your health, but your self-confidence, too. Walk, ride your bike, groove to the music, pump iron, putter in the garden... whatever. Just move.

I am _____
(fill in the blank)

>> **DO ONE THING.** We all have something (multiple somethings, probably) that we want to change or improve. Focus on one and get going. If it's a big goal, be sure to break it into little steps. Don't forget to celebrate your successes along the way.

>> **MIRROR WORK.** This was huge for me, back when my personal and professional lives were simultaneously circling the bowl. It's a simple exercise but not always easy. Go to a mirror, look yourself in the eye and say, "I love you." *THE HARDER IT IS TO DO THIS, THE MORE YOU NEED TO DO IT.* It took me months (I kid you not) to be able to reach the point where I didn't feel like a fake. Every time you see a mirror or even just a reflection of yourself, say those three words. And keep saying them till you mean it, no matter how long it takes.

>> **I AM** _____. I started the I Am Alphabet Game in my Time Tips time management group on Facebook and I could not believe how strongly it resonated with group members, who mostly were women. Here's how you do it: Each day, pick one letter of the alphabet. Use that letter to describe how you are or *HOW YOU WISH TO BE.* It must be a positive word and it must be *HOW YOU FEEL ABOUT YOURSELF* — not how others would describe you. None of this: "Well, my husband says I'm beautiful" or "My boss tells me I'm really efficient." Start with A, and complete the sentence, "I am _____." I am accomplished, active, accountable and so on. Not only is it fun, but the further you get in the alphabet, the easier it becomes — and the more empowered you feel.

CHAPTER 12
YOU ARE IN CONTROL OF YOU

There are very few feelings as debilitating as powerlessness, unable to grab hold of a situation and make it respond to you.

When you feel out of control, you can become depressed and unable to perform at work and at home.

How can we change that? By taking action. Action is the antidote to much of what ails us when we feel out of control, pushed around by people or unable to influence events.

The key thing to remember is that while we may not be in control of certain situations – say, the price of gasoline or a rude person on the phone – we most certainly are in control of how we react to them.

Can you lower the cost of fuel? Not directly, perhaps, but you can minimize the impact gasoline prices have on you. You can organize your errands so you're not making unnecessary trips. You can make sure your car's engine is running efficiently. You can buy a vehicle that gets better gas mileage, carpool, ride a bike and so on.

It may be more of a challenge to deal with the emotional backwash of someone who dumps on you, but you – and only you – are in charge of how that will affect you.

You can get angry, embarrassed, resentful, irate, hostile, withdrawn, sulky, annoyed, guilty and the rest of the range of negative emotions. I recommend that you allow yourself to feel those emotions instead of stuffing them; purge them from your system. The key is to turn those emotions around as quickly as you can.

Sound sappy?

Maybe – but if you have a choice between feeling bad and feeling good, which would you prefer?

It's hard to feel positive when someone is rude to you, but the truth is, you have no idea what prompted the rudeness. Almost certainly it has very little to do with you. You're just the most convenient whipping post, even if something you've said or done triggers the outburst.

COACHING REQUEST

Make a list at least once a week, daily if you're really under the gun:
» *WHAT ARE MY CHALLENGES?*
» *WHAT ARE MY OPPORTUNITIES?*
» *HOW CAN I CHANGE THE CHALLENGES INTO OPPORTUNITIES?*

CHAPTER 13
HAVE FAITH IN YOURSELF

Back when I was young and foolish, I told a prospective employer, "I can do just about anything, better than just about anyone."

Oh, the hubris! It's enough to make a grown woman blush.

But guess what? I got the job and my career took off. While the ensuing years have worn the sharp edges off that sense of invincibility, the hard core of that belief remains:

I have faith in me.

Having faith in yourself is the key in every aspect of life, especially as we get older and life throws curve balls at our heads and opens trenches at our feet. It's easy to forget that we can do just about anything if we put our mind – and heart and soul – to the task.

That's especially true these days, with so many women in transition. They have lost their jobs. Their spouses have moved out or died. Their children have moved on. Their health has become challenging.
What's left behind is often a sense of foreboding, a cringing in our souls as we wonder, "What's next?"
THE SHORT ANSWER: WHATEVER YOU WANT.

If you are finding yourself a bit short in the faith department, complete this request.

HAVE FAITH IN YOURSELF

COACHING REQUEST

» **THROW YOURSELF A PITY PARTY.** Go ahead with the whole "why me?" thing. Sob – the good, from-the-belly boo-hoo-hoos. Throw pillows. Scream. Cuss. Whatever helps you purge.

» **SET A TIME LIMIT.** Don't let your sob fest go on too long, because you've got things to do. This is a time not for giving up, but moving ahead to the future you deserve.

» **WHAT'S THE OPPORTUNITY?** Ask yourself: What can I create from this? I lost two-thirds of my client base not too long ago. And I rejoiced! It opened up time for me to complete this book and put it in your hands, for one thing. And it's not just me. One of my coaching clients has been out of work for seven years. Seven years! She decided it was time to take a good look at who and what she was – and wanted to be. She is now using her time to find out her life purpose, what she wants and how she can get it. It's a great opportunity for her and fills her with excitement and enthusiasm.

» **OUT OF WORK?** Look at the things you liked and didn't like in your former position. Start the hunt for something that's better suited for your personality. Give yourself the chance to shine.

» **WHAT ARE YOUR STRENGTHS?** You're tough. You're strong. You are a survivor, not a victim. That's how you got to where you are today. You know things now that you didn't know when you were younger. Let that work for you.

» **WHAT HAVE YOU LEARNED?** Not just job skills, although those are important, but in your life as a whole. What will you do differently with that knowledge?

» **YOU CAN'T CHANGE THE PAST.** But you can embrace your past as a learning tool. Use that knowledge help you use your present power and control to design your desired future.

» **GIVE YOURSELF PERMISSION TO DREAM.** Don't worry about what sounds whack-a-doodle or what other people will think. Screw that! Envision the way you want your life to be. Then go after it. Be bold! Life is too short to be mousy.

CHAPTER 14
MOTIVATION: ARE YOU AN INNY OR AN OUTY?

This isn't about your belly button – but it is about "navel gazing:" Does your motivation come from within or from the outside?

Motivation is vital when it comes to changing habits. If you are motivated from within, your chances of making big changes are much greater than if something outside is influencing you.

Look back at the times when you accomplished something huge. What set you down the path? What kept you moving when you wanted to quit?

If you moved forward because it was something you wanted for yourself, you most likely succeeded. Even then, it's no sure thing, particularly if you're doing it on your own without support.

But if you made changes in your life because a loved one nagged you or because "everyone is doing it," your shifts were probably short-lived. (Although research has shown that women, in particular, are often successfully motivated to do things others say they can't. We'll show them, by golly!)

Women struggle with finding what motivates them, what charges them up, because they have been encultured to put others first – children, grandchildren, helping other people. Or they believe it's something they will get – money, fame, adulation or respect.

If that latter one is you, you might want to rethink it. The best, most powerful motivation comes from feelings, not from objects, ideas, conditions, philosophical constructs or what you (or others) think you should do.

Here's an exercise that may help you find your motivation.

COACHING REQUEST

>> **DESCRIBE HOW YOU FEEL WHEN YOU HAVE IT.** "When I have _____, I feel _____." Not "feel like" or "feel that"; those aren't feelings you're expressing, but letting your brain speak instead of your heart.

>> **KEEP DRILLING DOWN** until you find the feeling that best describes your desired result. Choose liberated, overjoyed, satisfied, thrilled, free, lucky, thankful, energized or any of the dozens of other words that describe emotion. Use a thesaurus if you have to. Have fun with it!

>> **FOCUS ON POSITIVE RATHER THAN NEGATIVE FEELINGS.** It's so much more pleasant to embrace joy, satisfaction, gratitude and love. Knowing how you will feel will also be a great reminder during those times when you falter or wander off the path.

>> **RELEASE NEGATIVE EMOTIONS.** Fear, anger, envy, guilt, embarrassment, shame and bitterness – all are valid and real, and should be acknowledged. They are also toxic, limiting and unattractive, and they

30

consume a lot of energy that could be used to get you where you want to go. Recognize them and release them.

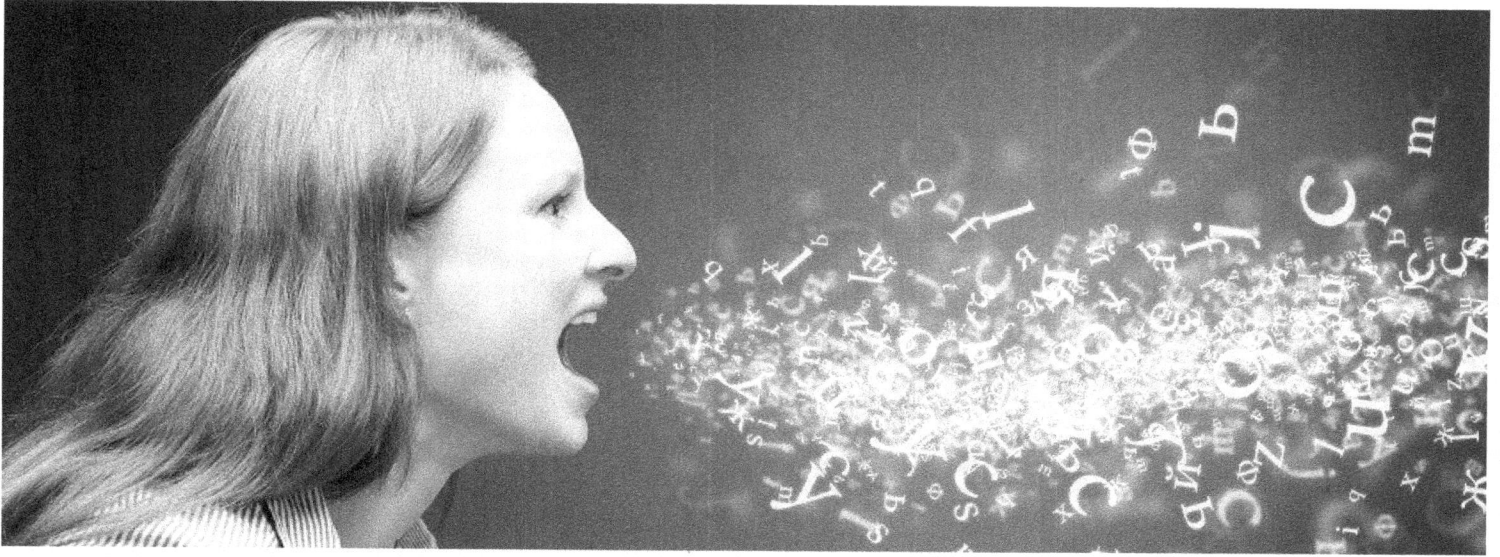

» *FULLY ENVISION YOUR DESIRED OUTCOME WHEN YOU ATTAIN IT.* While you're embracing the positive feelings that reaching your goal will provide, it also helps to envision it fully, with all your senses. Where will you be, physically? Who will be with you? How far in the future is it? What does your home look like? What kind of car will you be driving, if any? What will you look like? What kind of work will you be doing?

CHAPTER 15

FINDING THE VALUE IN CHANGE

The worst part about upheavals in our lives is the whole upheaval thing. Angst, uncertainty, doubt, second-guessing, stress, anger — you name it, you've gone through it.

Is there an upside? You bet! But few people want to think about that part. No one wants to even hear about that, because finding the gem in a pile of dung is the stuff of fables, the old "goodie two shoes" approach to life that can be so incredibly annoying.

Not only that, but slogging around in the slime is nasty and uncomfortable. It's much easier to wallow in the upheaval than to actually dig for the jewel. That's hard work.

But ah — the rewards! The first, most precious reward is that you will survive. As traumatic as the loss of a relationship, job, business or home can be, you will get through it. You've gotten through other crises before. You will again. Because that's who you are.

Your life does not get better by **chance**
It gets better by **change**

Another great reward is the opportunity to learn and grow. People become more creative and experimental when their lives smash into the reefs – they have no choice. They must do something.

More often than not, "something" is what turns out to be the real gem. They just didn't realize it was going to be at the bottom of a heap of nastiness, or that it was going to take that long to find it, or require that much work.

Understand this: Simple is not the same as easy. It kills me when I hear someone say, "Yeah, sounds simple but it's not easy."

Oh. Well. In that case, never mind. If it's going to be that much work, just forget about it. It must not be worth it. Right?

Wrong.

Where do we get the idea that everything has to be easy? Anything that has value has a price tag — whether it's money, time or effort.

To get started on your successful search for the gem, ask yourself these questions:

COACHING REQUEST

» **WHAT'S MY PATTERN?** How often has something like this happened to you? When was the last time? How did you get through it? Are you better or worse off as a result? How many times do you have to smack your head into the wall before you get that it will hurt every time?

» **AM I DRAWING AN ILLOGICAL CONCLUSION?** What is the very worst thing that could happen? Let your imagination romp. If it will not kill you or harm small children, "the very worst thing" that could happen is not only survivable, it may turn out to be the very best thing that ever happened to you.

» **WHAT SCARES ME THE MOST?** This is probably the thing you need to do most. Pay attention!

» **WHAT DO I HAVE TO LOSE?** When you have less to lose, you have less to lose. Take a chance!

» **WHAT HAVE I ALWAYS WANTED TO BE, DO OR HAVE?** This answer demands creativity and intuition. Be bold! Be wild and wacky. This is part of your journey to discovery. No one will hold you to it.

» **WHAT ARE THE GOOD THINGS THAT CAN OR WILL COME ABOUT AS A RESULT OF THIS CHANGE?** At the very least, you will learn something. At best, you won't do the same thing again. But even if you do, you're still further ahead than you were before.

» **WHAT AM I GRATEFUL FOR?** An attitude of gratitude can go a long way in your mental and emotional health department. Every time you start to wallow, quickly find something to be grateful for in your immediate surroundings. Repeat until the urge for self-pity goes away.

» **DO I CHOOSE TO BE POSITIVE ABOUT THIS CHANGE OR NEGATIVE?** You may not be able to halt the change, but you do have control about how you react to it. By keeping a positive outlook, you can make the search for the gem quicker... and a heck of a lot more pleasant.

CHAPTER 16
DEALING WITH TOXIC PEOPLE

DO ANY OF THESE PEOPLE SOUND FAMILIAR?

>> **THE BELITTLER:** Puts you down, and calls it "humor." Follows up with, "Aw, geez, can't you take a joke?"

>> **THE CONTROLLER:** "It's because I love you" is the excuse he uses for everything from calling or texting 20 times a day to isolating you from your friends to being at your side every free minute of the day to demanding to know who you've spoken to or seen when you were apart.

>> **THE MANIPULATOR:** Guilt is her most versatile weapon to get you to do what she wants. And she's really, really good at using it.

>> **THE DEPRESSED:** The glass is not just half empty, but bone dry and pulverized into dust, which always takes hours to clean up.

>> **THE VICTIM**: It's always someone else's fault, from missed planes to missed promotions.

Who's pulling **your** strings?

>> **THE CENTER OF THE UNIVERSE:** This is the opposite of The Victim but every bit as toxic. Everything is about her. She apologizes for everything, including bad weather, the economy and the bugs in your lawn.

>> **THE CONSPIRACY THEORIST:** Everyone's out to get him, except for you. And he's not entirely sure about you.

>> **THE MEGALOMANIAC:** No matter what you've suffered, he'll go you one (or two) better. Takes credit for all good things, avoids blame for the rest.

>> **THE NEEDY:** Always puts himself down to get other people to build him up.

And don't forget the Maudlin/Mean/Sloppy Drunk, the Man Who Knows Everything, the Unabashed Liar, the Congenitally Rude and the Parasite, among others.

If you have people like this in your life – run, don't walk! They are toxic.

They will drain your energy, mess with your head, play with your feelings and make you physically sick. They can pummel your self-esteem, make you question your own judgment and cause you to feel unworthy and "less than."

Whether they do it on purpose or subconsciously doesn't matter. The effect is the same – they drag you down.

Who needs it?

No one can make you feel bad without your permission, so take control. You do have a choice, especially in your personal relationships, such as friends, lovers, spouses and, yes, even nuclear family members.

It can be scary to stand up for what you want, but the payoff will be worth it (promise!). Ask yourself what's the worst that can happen, and then balance that against what you will gain.

And don't ever forget: It's about them, not about you. You are not to blame for the behavior of toxic people who depress you, deplete your good humor and suck away your energy. Nor do you have to put up with it.

As you go through the Coaching Request below, do you find yourself horrified by these actions? Do they give you a sinking feeling in your gut? If so, they are exactly what you need to pay the closest attention to.

COACHING REQUEST

» **SPEAK UP!** Say, "John, every time I see you, you're complaining. After spending time with you, I feel really down in the dumps and I don't want to put myself through that anymore."

» **ASK HIM TO CHANGE HIS BEHAVIOR, AT LEAST AROUND YOU.** If he agrees, and follows through, congratulations! May you live happily ever after. If, however, he backslides, remind him of your agreement. Eventually, when you reach the point where you cannot put up with it any more, then it's time for more drastic measures. You get to choose what that is.

» **BE PREPARED.** This kind of person will rarely recognize or acknowledge his own toxicity. When you call him out, be prepared to be ridiculed, cried upon, yelled at, viewed with wounded puppy eyes, threatened or any of an entire host of emotional reactions. Hang in there – don't let him bully you into backing down.

» **WHEN ALL ELSE FAILS, DROP THESE PEOPLE FROM YOUR LIFE.** Stay away from them. Don't call, write, visit or talk. And whatever you do, don't make excuses! Manipulators are especially adept at finding a way around excuses. If these are immediate family members, or those you must deal with through work, limit the time you spend with them.

» **TELL THEM WHY.** If they want to know why you've disappeared from their lives, tell the truth. It may be the best thing you can do for them. It will be easier if you've already had the conversation about their behavior. It's a little trickier to handle if the toxic people in your life are on the job.

» **IN THE WORKPLACE.** This has three parts:

1. **TALK TO THE HR DIRECTOR OR THE BOSS,** especially if the aggravation these people cause rises to the level of "hostile work environment." They'll want to know; believe me. This could very well be cause for legal action.

2. **LOOK FOR ANOTHER JOB.** Be sure you're willing to be chased away by one person.

3. **LIMIT YOUR INTERACTIONS.** If these people are merely annoying and you love what you're doing, be polite and professional, but don't accept lunch invitations. Make it clear you're too busy to chat and find other places to be and things to do when they drop in.

CHAPTER 17
PUTTING YOURSELF FIRST

WHAT PERCENTAGE OF YOUR LIFE ARE YOU LIVING FOR YOURSELF?

It's one of the questions I ask women as we embark on our coaching journey together, and the answer often comes as a surprise – or even an unpleasant shock – to the client.

The typical answer: 20%. Even those who start out at a higher percentage often will come back later and revise that figure downward – to their horror.

As enlightened, progressive and modern as our society has become, many women are still the primary caretakers of loved ones. These loved ones can be spouses or children or, increasingly, aged parents. Some even take care of friends.

Women are often caretakers in their work lives as well... the troubled colleague, the super busy co-worker who needs a hand, the newbie who's learning the ropes.

Sometimes they fill all these needs at once.

Moms fall into that a lot. They will do without, often for years, to make sure their kids are housed, fed and clothed – even if it means wearing rags themselves. That's their job, raising their children, and nothing is more important than that.

Of course, you don't have to be a parent to fall into the habit of putting other people first. Plenty of childless women find themselves in that role.

In some cases, self-sacrifice is a choice that comes from deeply held religious convictions. Many times, however, taking care of others is something we women do without thought, and in some situations, it comes at the expense of taking care of self.

36

Caretakers who decide to splurge on self-care – even with simple things like a hot bath, a solitary walk, reading a good book or watching a mindless TV show – often end up feeling guilty and selfish. From there, it's a short journey to feeling dissatisfied, restless, tired, depressed, sick, uneasy, resentful, angry or any of an entire host of negative emotions.

Does this sound familiar? If so, it's time to rethink taking care of you. Maybe even putting yourself first.

If following Coaching Request makes you uncomfortable, ticked off, in denial or outraged, ask yourself why. What you learn may be the start of a whole new appreciation of who you are, and what value you assign to yourself. And how much you are worth – to yourself.

COACHING REQUEST

ASK YOURSELF THESE QUESTIONS:

» Why is everyone else more important than me?

» Why are their needs more important than mine?

» How does being good to myself mean being bad to others?

» If I am doing the things that are right for me, how is that selfish?

» When I do what's right for me, am I doing it to hurt others?

» If other people feel hurt or inconvenienced when I do what's right for me, how is that my "fault"?

» Am I responsible for how other people feel?

» Did I consciously decide to give others the power to judge me, as selfish or as anything else?

» Do I want to spend the rest of my life doing what other people want me to do?

» If I am always putting others first – at the risk of neglecting myself – what message does that send to my children and others coming up behind me? What example am I setting?

» At what point do I say: "Enough!"?

IF NOTHING ELSE HERE PERSUADES YOU, THINK ABOUT THIS:

There is a reason why flight attendants tell you to put on your own oxygen mask first in case of emergency, even before your loved ones.
You are of no use to others if you are incapacitated.

CHAPTER 18
HOW TO STOP BEING A DOORMAT

HERE'S WHAT CHAPS MY CHEEKS: PEOPLE WHO TRY TO TAKE ADVANTAGE OF YOU.

Sadly, it happens all the time.

>> The sleazy mechanic who tells you on the phone the price to fix your car will be $147 and when you go to pick up your vehicle, it's $450, because he only told you the cost of the part. (Yes, this happened to me.)
>> The clerk who insists you only gave her $10 when you know good and well you gave her $20.
>> The client who says you screwed up, when you were just following her directions, and she wants you to redo the job – for free.

Happily, there are ways to handle situations like these. What follows are a few techniques that can help you learn how to stop people from manipulating you.

They all start with "No."

Just that one word.

Do not give a reason or an excuse because people who are trying to take advantage of you will always find a way around them.

If you feel you need to elaborate, feel free to say, "No, I can't do that." Or "No, I wish I could." Or, if you feel you must, "No, I'm sorry. I can't."

Example:

John: "I would really appreciate it if you could take care of my dog while I'm on vacation."

You: "Oh, John, I would love to, but I don't have the time."

John: "Sure you do! Spot only needs to go out twice a day. You can do that! You work from home."

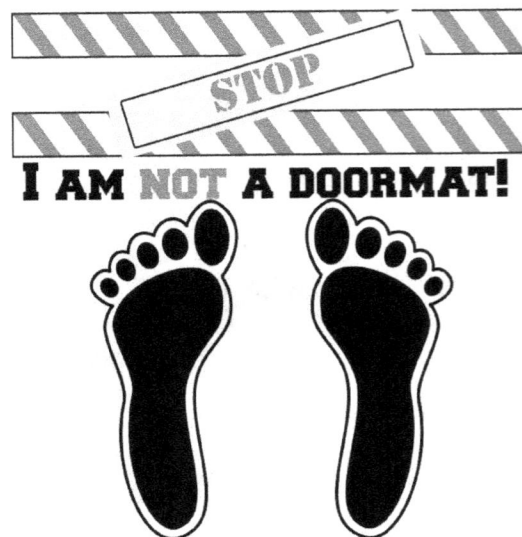

HERE YOU HAVE TWO CHOICES:

1. You can get into a long explanation and possible argument with John justifying your decision. The problem with this solution is that by doing this, you give John the right to judge – and thereby control – your behavior.

2. You can cave in and hate yourself. As a result, you end up losing a piece of your self-respect and resenting John for taking advantage of you.

Luckily, there is a third alternative: Saying no – and sticking to it – by using three of my favorite basic assertive-language techniques, Broken Record, Fogging and Negative Assertion.

These techniques come from the classic assertiveness book, *When I Say No, I Feel Guilty*, by Manuel J. Smith, Ph.D.

» **BROKEN RECORD.** Repeat yourself, as many times as necessary, to get the point across.

» **FOGGING.** Agree with your critic, which will drive them crazy (part of the fun, honestly), but stick to your guns.

» **NEGATIVE ASSERTION.** Accept the truth in the critical comment.

HERE'S HOW THAT CONVERSATION COULD GO USING THESE ASSERTIVENESS TECHNIQUES.

JOHN: "I would really appreciate it if you could take care of my dog while I'm on vacation."

YOU: "Oh, John, I would love to help out, but I can't."

JOHN: "What do you mean, you can't? Of course you can! You work from home, for crying out loud!"

YOU: "You're right, I do work from home." (Fogging)

JOHN: "Great! Let me give you my key so you can take care of him."

YOU: "Keep the key, John; I can't take care of Spot for you." (Broken Record)

JOHN: "I can't believe you're doing this to me! I know you took care of Fred's cat when he was called out of town."

YOU: "I did, didn't I?" (Fogging, Negative Assertion) "Unfortunately, I can't take care of Spot when you go on vacation." (Broken Record)

JOHN: "You are a crappy neighbor! Don't ever ask me for a favor, because I'll tell you where to stick it!"

YOU: "You could be right; I could be a better neighbor." (Fogging)

JOHN: "A good neighbor would help out."

YOU: "I guess I'm just a lousy neighbor then, because I can't take care of Spot." (Fogging, Broken Record)

At that point, what else can he do? He's criticized you and called you names and all the while he's been swinging at fog. He never lands a punch because you don't give him a hard surface to strike.

He goes away mad – but he does go away. Praise be! And you've gotten yourself out of an obligation you didn't want, held on to your self-esteem, and kept control of your time (and your temper). What's not to like?

Your relationship with John may be chilly going forward, but does that matter? John has demonstrated that your needs (and your feelings) are less important than his, and that he will say whatever he thinks will work to get what he wants. I don't know about you, but this is not someone I want to pal around with.

How do you know if you're giving up your personal power? Check your gut. If you're feeling angry, resentful, guilty, trapped, put upon, backed into a corner or out of control, you probably are being manipulated.

COACHING REQUEST

>> ***FIND A LOW-RISK SITUATION AND PRACTICE ASSERTIVE BEHAVIOR.*** Try my personal favorite — telemarketers. Instead of not answering the phone or hanging up on them, take the call and practice these techniques. The more you do, the more comfortable you'll feel doing it. Then move on to those situations that really count!

CHAPTER 19
HOW TO STOP BEING A BAD-LUCK MAGNET

Are you a "bad luck" magnet? Do you expect the worst, so you won't be disappointed?

Or does nearly everything go your way? Do you see the bright side in everything that happens to you?

Either way, I'd bet that you get exactly what you expect.

It's the Law of Attraction, based on the law of physics that states that whatever energy we put out – negative or positive – is matched by more of the same.

Consider the tuning fork, a simple metal two-pronged fork whose tines resonate at a specific musical pitch when struck against a surface.

Take a thousand tuning forks, all set to vibrate at the different frequencies, and put them in a stadium. Strike one fork – the A, for example – and all the other A's in the stadium will resonate.

Not the B-flats or C's... just the A's.

Here's another example that's a little closer to home.

Our alarm doesn't go off and our first thought is, "Oh, man, is THIS going to be a rotten day!"

Sure enough, it is.

We stub our toe getting out of bed, we burn the toast, we lose our keys, the car has a flat, some bum steals that coveted parking space and on and on. We expect an awful day and that's precisely what we get.

To bring "good luck" or "good karma" into our lives, we need to change the way we feel about what's happening to us, and how we express it to ourselves.

The best way to start is to remove these three words from our vocabulary: "Don't," "not" and "no."

Yes, yes, I know. I just told you in the last chapter to say "no" when people are pushing you around (or trying to!). Here's the difference:

Learning how to say "no" to others is important to setting and maintaining boundaries, to asking for – and getting – what you want.

Saying "no" to yourself, on the other hand, is negative and self-limiting.

Here's another example. If you say to your pet, "No treat," what word is it going to hear? Try a Google search on "no football," and of the nearly 9 million results you get, nearly 9 million will be on virtually everything but (you guessed it) "no football."

The same thing applies to the positive and negative energy you produce.

What's your mindset? Scarcity – "need to" Abundance – "want to"

If you say, " don't want to lose this account; I don't want to cry in front of the boss; I don't want to be broke," the message – the energy – you're sending out is "lose," "cry" and "broke." That, too, is what your brain is hearing and its job is to organize your life around what you tell it is important.

By focusing on your "don't wants," that's exactly what you'll get back... what you don't want.

When you change the words, you also will change the energy, the message to your brain and your mood.

"I want this to keep and grow this account. I want to be calm. I want my life to be filled with abundance." Notice that use "want" instead of "need." "Want" is a word of abundance; "need" is a word of scarcity. By using "need," you are telling your brain to seek out the bare minimum. You want as much as possible! Not only that, it just feels better to want things than to need them.

The moment you shift your energy to the positive is the moment you start to attract the positive to your life.

Here's a three-step formula to do just that.

COACHING REQUEST

>> **IDENTIFY YOUR DESIRE.** We women are not good at this; we're better at saying what we don't want. But we can use our "don't wants" as a starting place. If you hate your job, for example, try imagining your perfect job. What kind of work would you do? Who are the people you would work with? How much money would you make? What would your environment look like? And most of all, how would it feel to have that perfect position?

>> **GIVE WHAT YOU WANT ATTENTION, ENERGY AND FOCUS.** The Law of Attraction says: "You attract to yourself whatever you give your attention and energy to, whether wanted or unwanted."

>> **ALLOW IT.** Allowing is the absence of doubt, which is negative energy. It's the most important step of the three – and the most challenging. It really is OK to want things for yourself. It's not selfish and you deserve it. So allow it into your life.

CHAPTER 20
WHEN ADULT KIDS MOOCH

A whopping 36% of America's adult children age 18-31 are living with their parents. "Why" doesn't matter for our purposes. What matters is how to deal with perfectly able kids whose sense of entitlement is preventing you from having a happy, relaxed home life.

The phrasing used in the following Coaching Request comes from one of my coaching clients, who wanted her son to contribute financially.

COACHING REQUEST

» **PICK A TIME AND PLACE FOR THE CONVERSATION.** Being in a public place could keep down the histrionics, or could ratchet them up. Use your best judgment.

» **TELL HIM HOW YOU FEEL WITH AN "I" STATEMENT.** For example, "I feel taken advantage of when you don't contribute to any of the household expenses."

» **TELL HIM WHAT YOU WANT.** "I want you to start paying $100 a week for room and board." (Yes, you're allowed to want things, and to say them out loud.)

» **PREPARE AND PRACTICE.** If you can, map out in advance with a friend or a coach how the conversation is likely to go. Do some role-playing, so you'll have a response to whatever they are likely to say. Have your coach exaggerate the reaction you expect so you can get used to dealing with the worst-case scenario. Practice!

» **DEAL WITH THE PUSHBACK.** You're likely to get pushback and that's when it's easy to get sidetracked. Stay focused! Keep bringing the conversation back around to what you want: "I do love you, and I want you to start paying some of the expenses around the house." This is an example of the "Broken Record" assertiveness technique, because you may have to repeat it many times.

» **OUTLINE THE CONSEQUENCES.** "If you don't pay $100 a week, you'll have to move out of the house by___."

» **ASK FOR HIS AGREEMENT.** If he refuses, follow through. Boot him out. If he agrees, and then fails to follow through, boot him out.

CHAPTER 21
HOW TO STOP BEING THE CENTER OF THE UNIVERSE

"But what will people think of me?"

I'm amazed at the number of women – myself included, sometimes – who hold themselves back because they're worried about what other people think of them.

Take the woman who says training other people can be misinterpreted as being "pushy," while the same quality exhibited by men would be considered "mentoring."

Uh-huh. And?

There is a long list of behaviors that, when applied to men, are deemed positive and when used to describe women... well, not so much. And "pushy" is the kindest one I can think of.

So what?

As with anything in life, we have a choice. We can get resentful (and I have been) that women are denigrated for displaying the exact same traits as men. If we're not careful, we can get stuck here and poison our own life.

Or we can accept the fact that we have no control over what people think of us, shrug and move on.

A large part of moving forward is just not giving a damn about what others think. Caring too much about other people's opinions can hold you back from being the best version of yourself.

HERE'S WHERE I NOTE SOME QUALIFIERS – A LIST, IN DESCENDING ORDER, OF PEOPLE WHOSE OPINIONS OF YOU CARRY WEIGHT:

» Immediate family members, including spouse, kids, parents and so on
» Close friends
» Your boss/clients
» Your employees and other business associates

I'm not saying you should 100% buy in to their opinions, because you are your own person and should do what works best for you (even if it means leaving a job or a relationship). Listen to see if their views have merit, understand that they have skin in the game and make your own judgments and decisions.

But if you're worried about what some random stranger on the street thinks of you, or the guy in line with you at Starbucks, or someone you just met at a party, then it's time to give yourself a good shake and figure out why your self-esteem is in the dumper.

> ## "We would worry less about what others think of us if we realized how seldom they do."
> ### Ethel Barrett

We can live our lives trying to be all things to all people and we will fail miserably. And die miserably, too. I can't imagine a more stress- and angst-filled life.

Want to desensitize yourself to what other people think of you? Read on!

COACHING REQUEST

» *CURB YOUR IMAGINATION.* "Oh my God! If I wear those socks, everyone will think I'm color blind!" Or "I just know everyone will hate my presentation and think I'm an idiot." Hold your horses, cowgirl! First, you need to learn how to stop being the center of the universe. Not everyone's focus is on your clothing color or pattern, or how many times you stumble during your speech. That's kind of big-headed of you, don't you think? Second, think it through – there are going to be some people who absolutely love purple and green argyle and some people who hate it. There will be some people who snore through your report and others who will be riveted. Stop thinking in absolutes and cut yourself some slack.

» *BE OK WITH NOT KNOWING WHAT PEOPLE THINK.* You may be surprised at how little people actually think about you – or, in the immortal words of writer Ethel Barrett, *"WE WOULD WORRY LESS ABOUT WHAT OTHERS THINK OF US IF WE REALIZED HOW SELDOM THEY DO."*

» *ACCEPT THAT YOU HAVE NO CONTROL OVER HOW OTHER PEOPLE PERCEIVE YOU.* At the very least, their opinions are based on incomplete information. They have no idea what's going on in your life, head and heart; even those closest to you are clueless to a degree. And truly, is it their business? Some people will judge you based on your skin color (or hair color, as I found out recently), your sex, age, educational background, the car you drive and so on. Should we let those opinions determine our actions and our feelings of self-worth? I don't think so. People's perceptions are more about them than us and have at least as much to do with what's going on in their own lives.

» *BE COMFORTABLE IN YOUR OWN SKIN.* Everyone has quirks and foibles. Everyone has habits and perspectives. Everyone is unique. The more comfortable we are with ourselves, the less other people's opinions of us matter. And for extra bonus points – the less judgmental we become as well.

» *ASK YOURSELF: WHAT WOULD MY LIFE LOOK LIKE IF I DIDN'T CARE ABOUT THE OPINIONS OF OTHERS?* More importantly, how would it feel to live your life unburdened by the opinions and expectations of others? Maybe you'd learn salsa, if you didn't care about what people thought as you staggered through the dance steps. Maybe you'd buy a house in the mountains and open a B&B, if you didn't care that people thought you were nuts. Maybe you'd learn the tuba, or build websites, or sail around the world. And you'd love every minute of it, because it's what you chose to do.

CHAPTER 22
HANDLING CRITICISM

It's easy to avoid criticism. Aristotle figured it out centuries ago. "To avoid criticism say nothing, do nothing, be nothing."

That sounds a lot like being dead, and since we know that even death is no protection against criticism, it makes sense to learn how to accept criticism, reframe it and deal with it.

Here are some tips that should help.

COACHING REQUEST

>> **KNOW YOURSELF.** When you fully understand who you are and understand your strengths and weaknesses, it will be much easier to examine criticism on its merits. It's your job to figure out if negative comments are true – and that's best done from a place of personal strength, self-awareness and honesty. (This will also keep you from being easily swayed by flattery, too.)

>> **STEP BACK.** It's so easy to take offense at criticism, particularly if it is directed at something you believe in passionately. It may even be a personal attack, but nothing is gained by reacting emotionally. Approach the criticism with a cool head and you may learn something that will help you improve. Or it may help you decide who you need to avoid in the future. That's a win-win, in my view.

>> **CONSIDER THE SOURCE.** Who is the critic? What's the motivation? Is it jealousy? Ignorance? Is it a competitor – for your job, your business or your sweetheart's affection? Even those who love you best can be motivated by their own needs and desires, not what's in your best interest. Someone who criticizes you for leaving one job for another, for example, may want to keep you in place for reasons of their own.

>> **HOW WAS THE CRITICISM DELIVERED?** Was it given in anger? Carelessly? Deliberately hurtful? Even the best-intentioned people can feel awkward in offering feedback, so the way it's presented may not be phrased the best way. Look for intent first, content second.

>> **LISTEN.** Just because someone was hurtful doesn't mean they're wrong. Let those comments "age" past the desire to retaliate. If you feel you must respond, be non-committal: "You may have a point." "That's something to consider." "I understand what you're saying." None of these agrees with the criticism – they merely tell the other person that you're hearing them.

>> **CHECK IT OUT.** Take that feedback to someone you know and trust – and not necessarily someone who agrees with you all the time. Get their reaction.

>> **REFRAME IT.** Once you've decided there is merit in the criticism, use it as an opportunity to learn and grow. Sometimes it requires a hard knock to make that happen.

>> **ADMIT IT.** If you've done something demonstrably wrong, admit it. Most people are kind and generous and are willing to forgive a mistake. However, if it's a judgment of you as a person instead of your actions, go back to "consider the source."

» **TRUST YOURSELF.** If, after going through all this, you feel the criticism was unwarranted, let it go. You can approach it from one of two ways: (1) agree to disagree or (2) recognize that there are some people whose opinions aren't worth spit on the sidewalk.

Part 2 CAREER

CHAPTER 23
FINDING YOUR IDEAL JOB

Are you still searching for the perfect job?

Here's an exercise for you to complete in the next week to help you come up with a "development commitment" plan.

This plan works whether you are looking for a new job, want to strike off on your own or want to make any type of changes in your life.

COACHING REQUEST

» **CREATE A DOCUMENT WITH THREE COLUMNS.**
» At the top of Column 1, write: "Things I have in my job now, or in past jobs, that I don't want in my next job."
» On Column 2: "Things I have in my job now, or in past jobs, that I want in my next job."
» Column 3: "Things I haven't had in any job that I want as part of my next job."
» **FILL IN ALL THE BLANKS.** These things can be anything, including job duties, work environment, type of people in your office, type of customers you work with, hours worked, wages, dress code, benefits, respect from your boss or coworkers – whatever comes to mind.
» **ADD OR DELETE THROUGHOUT THE WEEK.**
» **HIGHLIGHT THOSE ITEMS THAT SPEAK LOUDEST TO YOU.** Which are the most important to have... or not have... in your next job? Don't worry about setting goals at this point; this is merely a tool to help you more clearly identify what you do and do not want. (You will find more about setting goals elsewhere)
» **AT THE END OF THE WEEK,** go to the third column and put a minus sign in front of those items that require development. They could be moving to a new location or getting more education or training.
» **IDENTIFY FIVE NON-NEGOTIABLE ITEMS IN THE LAST COLUMN.** Mark them with a plus sign. Go with your gut; don't let the expectations and desires of others rule your thinking. And watch out for self-talk that includes words like "can't," "won't," "impossible," "stupid," "illogical," "selfish," "unrealistic" and the rest of those judgmental terms. This is about what you want, not what others want.

CHAPTER 24

NEGOTIATING FOR WHAT YOU WANT

When my business mentor told me I should do a webinar on negotiation skills for women, I panicked. Oh my God, I said, I don't know ANYTHING about negotiations!

Of course, that was a big fat lie.

I negotiate all the time – and so do you. If you've ever held a management position and asked for more resources, you've negotiated. If you have kids who want something extra, you've negotiated. If you've ever bought a car, you've negotiated. If you've ever hired a contractor, you've negotiated.

So why do we women freak out when we think of negotiations? It's because we've been taught to be nice, accommodating, agreeable, modest, sweet and easy-going.

In the workplace, we feel that if we talk about our accomplishments, it will come across as bragging. And too many of us believe that if we just work hard, we will be recognized and rewarded appropriately.

Don't believe everything you think.

Imagine this scenario: Two equally qualified people want a promotion to a top job. One person advocates for herself, talking about her accomplishments, her vision for the position and how she can take the company to the next level, with supporting facts and passion. The other person sits back and waits to be recognized for her work

Who do you think will get that position?

Especially in a big company, it is wishful and dangerous thinking to believe that a busy manager, with many direct reports, is going to be intimately familiar with the accomplishments of everyone in his department, or intuit that a particular employee is interested in a leadership position.

It's like the wife who hopes and dreams of getting a special Valentine's Day present, but never says anything – and then gets miffed when her husband gives her a vacuum cleaner.

WHY IS IT IMPORTANT TO KNOW HOW TO NEGOTIATE?

>> **THE FEMALE DISADVANTAGE.** Women earn only 77 cents for every dollar paid to men – right off the top. By the time they are 50, that number drops to about 50 cents. To make matters worse, there also is the Mommy Penalty.

>> **THE MOMMY PENALTY.** A recent study reported by the Harvard Business School showed that mothers were offered $11,000 less in salary when a group of test interviewers was given the choice between an equally qualified man and woman. There was no pay disparity when the interviewers learned that the man had children.

» THE RETIREMENT PINCH. Women with children on average spend about half the time in the workforce as men do. As a result, their retirement funds, Social Security benefits and pension plans are commensurately less. Throw in the 50% divorce rate, add in women's longer lifespans and top it off with reduced Social Security widows' benefits and it becomes painfully clear that relying on your spouse or significant other is a lousy financial plan.

Clearly, women need to advocate for themselves — to negotiate better salaries, titles and benefits. And the sooner they learn those skills and put them to good use, the better.

Beyond the financial reasons why women need to learn negotiation skills, there are professional benefits, too.

You will never advance very far — never even learn how far you can go — if you can't effectively advocate for yourself. Negotiation skills pay massive personal benefits, too, in improved self-esteem, ability to communicate clearly and think quickly on your feet.

They help you learn how to deal with rejection and bounce back; school your emotions so they work for you instead of against you; and help you be persistent.

For those of us who are afraid of rejection, remember that "no" is not fatal. Heck, sometimes "no" isn't even "no" — just "not yet." There are many legitimate factors that could lead to a negative answer — budgetary, timing, growth plans — things you are completely unaware of but still come into play.
To get your head in the right place, find a handful of people who you can trust to be honest with you and ask them this: What two things do they consider to be your gifts? And in what two areas do they think you are holding yourself back?

Ha! You thought I'd talk about your weaknesses, didn't you? No way! This is not about your skill set, it's about your mindset.

You also need to rev yourself up by giving yourself permission. You are allowed to want things for yourself. Really. It's not selfish; it's a sign of self-love.

And if you find yourself saying, "I should want..." stop right there. You are probably repeating someone else's expectations of you. Live your life, not someone else's version of what it should be.

If you want to get more, here are some tips to help make your negotiations successful.

COACHING REQUEST

>> **DO YOUR HOMEWORK.** Whether it is a raise, a promotion, more clients or whatever else it is you want, do your research, online or through your network. Find out what other people are making in your job title, industry and locale. If you want more clients, see where they hang out and go hang out with them.

>> **ASSIGN VALUE.** It can be how much business you've brought in the last year. It can be how much more business your clients have landed since hiring you. If you can't point to a bottom-line improvement, assign value to additional responsibilities you've taken on, how many more accounts you've got in your portfolio, how many people you have hired/trained. Be creative.

>> **AIM HIGH.** Whatever you want, add another 30% – just to make up the average difference between what men and women earn. Be sure your facts support the amount.

>> **PREPARE FOUR OPTIONS.** The last one should be "walk away." Write them down and take them into your meeting.

>> **PRACTICE, PRACTICE, PRACTICE.** Find a coach, friend, family member – anyone who can sit with you and practice your pitch. Tell your practice partner how you expect the other person to react and ask them to exaggerate it. It will help you better organize your thinking and shore up any places that need additional work. Run through it as many times as you need until you feel confident and comfortable.

>> **KEEP THE CONVERSATION FOCUSED ON THE ISSUES.** This is not personal.

>> **WEAR A POWER OUTFIT.** If you don't own one, go shopping and charge it off as a business expense. It should be well-made and fit perfectly (get it tailored, if necessary). Most importantly, it should make you feel fabulous when you put it on.

>> **YOU START THE NEGOTIATIONS.** The person who talks numbers first is setting the amount around which the discussion will revolve. It's easier to negotiate down from, let's say, $100,000 than up from $50,000.

>> **SIT SIDE BY SIDE.** If your counterpart is behind a desk (a power position) and you're invited to sit in a chair on the other side, move your chair to help establish a level playing field.

>> **DON'T NOD.** Women nod to show they've heard; men nod to show agreement. Don't send the wrong non-verbal message.

>> **DON'T ACCEPT THE FIRST OFFER.** That's why they call it "negotiations."

>> **LEAVE OUT WEASEL WORDS AND PHRASES.** "Feel," "think" and "believe" are the worst. "I think I deserve a raise"? No. You KNOW you deserve a raise. You "think" you can do the job? You "believe" you're qualified? Come on, girl – get with it! Thinking, feeling and believing have no place in a negotiation. Own it.

>> **DON'T SAY THESE THINGS EITHER.** Other phrases you never want to hear coming out of your mouth (just typing these give me the willies):

"I'm not an expert but…"

"I could be wrong…"

"This is probably silly, but…"

"If you can afford it."

"I know times are tough."

>> **SPEAK IN DECLARATIVE SENTENCES.** Don't allow your voice to go up at the end of each sentence. It makes you sound wishy-washy and women do this way too much.

» **ZIP IT.** After you lay out what you want and make your fact-based case for it, keep quiet for 7 seconds. It will show you mean what you say.

» **DON'T LET YOUR EMOTIONS OVERWHELM YOU.** Having all your numbers in hand will keep you on an even keel during the discussion. Don't be bullied, pulled off track or respond to attacks that are designed deliberately to get your goat. Don't give him/her the satisfaction. You are in charge of you.

» **SIT IN AN UNCOMFORTABLE CHAIR.** It will help you stay alert. Just don't fidget!

For more information, be sure to check out the accompanying workbook.

CHAPTER 25
YOU'RE THE BOSS – ACT LIKE IT

I got this email from one of the women in one of my time management webinars, and I don't know whether to weep, scream, pull out my hair or all three.

She writes: "My team consists of 3 people other than me. I really work by deadlines. I have never missed a deadline yet. Therefore, people rely on me in terms of critical duties.

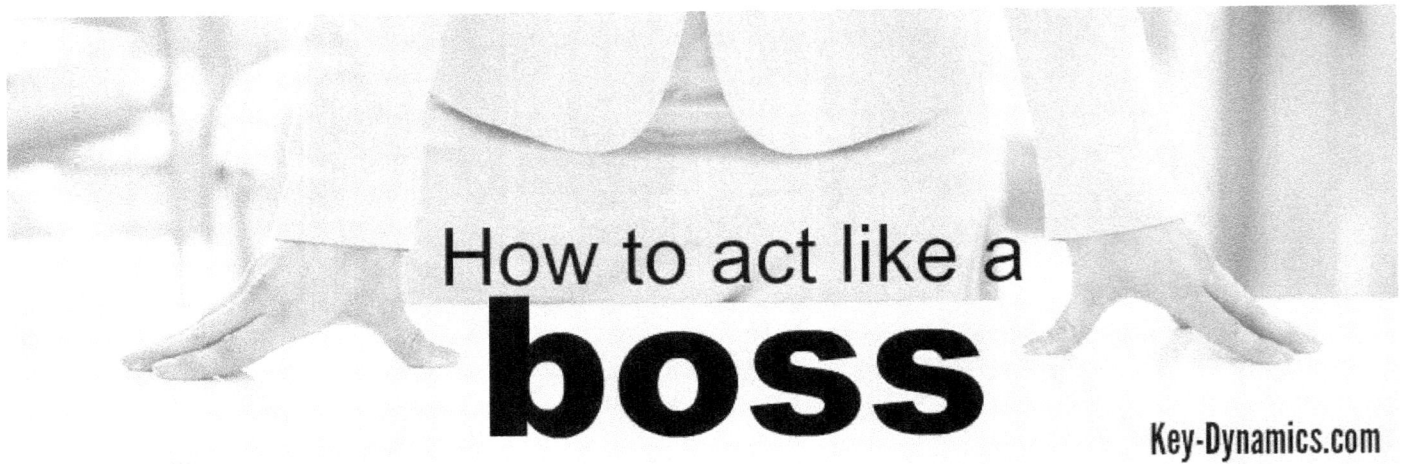

How to act like a **boss**

Key-Dynamics.com

"Whenever a team member complains about the intense conditions of his job, I share his duties to lessen his burden. Whenever the office needs a report to be submitted to any high-level person, I write those reports. Whenever something has to be written or prepared for the first time, I'm the person to do that. But I also have my routine jobs that I should perform.

"In the end, I don't get time to breathe. I work at home, I work on the weekends. I put my priorities back all the time. (For example, I can't finish my master's thesis, because I bring the job home.)

"I don't know how to say no. Because I feel like saying no is equal to irresponsibility. I also cannot make a person finish his job by using my position as a manager because I use empathy so much and feel sympathy toward that person. I don't know how to change my habits.

"Thank you very much for being there and making me feel like I'm not alone in this. I thank God for small miracles :)"

• • •

Oh my! There is so much here and it all wrenches my heart. But I will say this: Jane (not her real name) is not alone. Not even for a minute. There are many, many women in the same spot as she is.

» She has no boundaries
» She always puts herself last
» She shies away from using her authority to make changes in the workplace

All of these challenges can be turned into opportunities, not just for Jane but for the people she supervises. I will not get into setting boundaries, becoming more assertive, how to handle manipulative behavior or any of that because that is covered elsewhere in this book.

Instead, let's talk about Jane's situation from a global management standpoint. If you are also in her situation, keep in mind this key fact: You are the supervisor.

Sometimes you have to make hard choices as a boss. This is why you get paid more (hopefully) than your team members. It is your job to make sure your employees are doing their work, not doing it for them.

Taking on their work, on top of yours, is doing no one any favors and ultimately it is harming the company. You might even say you're cheating the company because you are not doing the job you were hired to do.

If you find yourself in Jane's spot, I offer the following:

COACHING REQUEST

» **PROVIDE TRAINING.** If you have a whiny employee who cannot handle the "intense conditions of his job," the first option is always to provide more training.

» **INSTITUTE PROGRESSIVE DISCIPLINE.** Give him specific goals to achieve over a limited period. Make sure he knows, up front, that you want him to succeed and if he doesn't, his job is at stake.

» **REVIEW HIS PERFORMANCE REGULARLY.** If he hasn't met his goals, you've got one final option.

» **FIRE HIM.** This isn't easy or pleasant, particularly if you are new at supervision. But know that up to this point, you have done everything in your power – shy of doing his job for him – to help him succeed. You can be as sympathetic as you like, but he is responsible for his own success, just as you are responsible for your own. You will be doing him a favor by letting him find employment better suited to his temperament. You will be happier, your team will respect you and you can find someone who is a better fit for the job.

» **DELEGATE.** Focus on those things only you can do – and for which you were hired. Pass along the paperwork, if possible, to someone else. Train these employees, if they need it. Be available to answer questions. Pay close attention to their work and show them how they can improve. Be appreciative and generous with your praise. This is how you develop your team members, and improve their value to the company.

CHAPTER 26
STOP MICROMANAGING

Office workers are interrupted on average every 3 minutes.

Yes. Every 3 minutes.

The biggest transgressor? The boss.

When I offered some tips online on how to manage interruptions, one woman wrote, "Easier said than done, when [we] are interrupted by management who want what they want when they want it. If interruptions are every two minutes, and last 1 minute apiece, half of the office worker's day is wasted."

Actually, it can be more like 6 hours a day, not 4, according to some efficiency experts. Not only do workplace interruptions stop the normal flow of business, they add more time – about 23 minutes – to getting the original tasks done as employees try to pick up where they left off.

This amounts to a total loss to the U.S. economy of about $1 TRILLION a year. That's no way to run a business.

As the boss, it's your responsibility to see that your employees have a workplace that is conducive to... well... work. If you're not managing that properly, then you're not doing your job.

You may need to have some heart-to-heart conversations. So be it. It's better for your company culture and employee morale than having you watch everyone like a hawk. And you can learn how to have those conversations, if you haven't already been trained.

Culling the deadwood is vital if you want to retain (or improve) the level of respect your employees have for you. Because I can assure you your employees know exactly who the slackers are and what they're getting away with.

COACHING REQUEST

» **GIVE PEOPLE THE TOOLS THEY NEED.** In the case of new employees, make sure they have a clear understanding of what the job entails and they are trained to do it. Trying to guess what makes you happy is a huge time-waster.

» **DEAL WITH THE SLACKERS.** If you have employees who need to be checked on all the time, you need to create performance plans for them that include specific goals and timelines by which they need to be accomplished. Be clear that failure to perform will result in the loss of their jobs.

» **ASK FOR FEEDBACK.** Instead of badgering your employees every few minutes – or allowing that to happen – ask them what ideas they have for a better system. You might be surprised at what you learn. It also helps to ask your employees how long they think a task will take to complete. They are your front line – chances are they have a better handle on such nitty-gritty details than you do.

» **CREATE "INSIDE TIME" AGREEMENTS.** Joan has a major report to finish by 5 p.m. today and it will take 2 hours to complete. Give her the two hours she needs – let her close the door (if she has one), turn off the phone, ignore emails and so on. If she doesn't have a door, have her put up a sign that says, "Do not interrupt between the hours of 1-3 p.m." Let everyone know she has your permission to do so. Then leave her alone.

» **ESTABLISH REGULAR MEETING TIMES.** You're the manager; you need to know how everything is going in your department or your company. Meetings are frequently reviled but properly run, they can provide you with all the information you need without hovering over your employees. The more people involved in the meeting, the more important it is to have an agenda with a strict start and end time. One-on-one meetings can be less formal, but still have a time limit and be specific about the topics you want to discuss. No going off the reservation. Everyone has stuff that needs to be done, including you.

» **GET OVER YOURSELF.** If you're one of those types of managers who is set in your ways, think you know it all and will not even listen to suggestions, you need to ask yourself, "Am I in the right job? Do I need more training?"

CHAPTER 27
WHEN MEETINGS GO BAD

If you feel as if you spend your entire working life in meetings, you're not far off the mark.

Estimate range from six hours for managers of small- to medium-sized companies to a staggering 30 hours a week for CEOs of major corporations. This does not count meeting prep time.

That's a lot of money and talent tied up – and too often frittered away – when meetings go bad.

Your experience may be different, but there is nothing inherently wrong with meetings.

They can lead to greater understanding and buy-in of company goals. They can draw out the best from each participant, and distill that experience and knowledge into new products, services and systems.

Meetings can bring together diverse points of view and strengthen teamwork. They can fire up lackluster work groups and improve performance.

Does it make you weep to think that you've never been part of a meeting like that? They do exist. Best of all, you can create them yourself!

The key is structure. That's what allows the magic to occur.

COACHING REQUEST

>> **START WITH A PURPOSE.** Why are you having the meeting? What do you want to accomplish? Be clear in your own mind before you call your meeting.
>> **CREATE AN AGENDA.** What will be discussed? Include the start and end times. This is mandatory.
>> **DETERMINE WHO ABSOLUTELY MUST BE THERE.** Does every soul who works in the company need to be there? Are there people outside the firm – vendors or contractors, perhaps — who should also be invited? When it comes to process/working meetings, as opposed to informational meetings, the

fewer people the better. That way, everyone gets the chance to participate and the possibility of chaos decreases.

» **GIVE PARTICIPANTS WHAT THEY NEED – AND PLENTY OF NOTICE.** Preparing for a meeting is crucial if you want quality participation. One of the reasons meetings go bad is because participants don't do their homework and way too much time is wasted bringing the laggards up to speed. To prevent that, given them the materials the need and tell attendees that you expect them to come ready to work.

» **MAKE SURE YOU'RE MEETING IN THE RIGHT PLACE.** Does the site have the facilities and equipment you need? Is it set up properly? Is there good ventilation? If it's a working session, is there enough room for people to spread out comfortably?

» **START ON TIME.** Respect your participants' time. Start when you said you would.

» **HAVE A RECORDER.** This person can take notes or tape the meeting, but someone needs to capture the details. By details, I don't mean a word-for-word transcription of who said what. Generally, all you need to do is include what decisions were made and who is to do what by when.

» **THE CHAIRMAN'S ROLE.** Too many meeting chairmen believe their job is to force everyone to do what he wants done. Nope. The chairman's job is to encourage everyone to participate, recognize that participation, rein in the floor-hogs, keep an eye on the clock and the agenda, and move the discussion forward in an orderly fashion – all with diplomacy, strength and tact. A good chairman will keep asking, "What else?" to get at all possible solutions.

» **RECAP.** A great meeting ends with a general recap of what has been decided – what steps have to be taken, who is responsible for making it happen, a deadline by which it must be accomplished and setting a date for the next meeting to share and measure progress.

CHAPTER 28
LEADERSHIP

When you think about leadership, what – or who – comes to mind?

Is the leader the top guy on the corporate ladder? The chairwoman of the Board of Directors? The man speaking from the pulpit? Someone who runs the biggest charity in town?

In a nutshell, leaders are people who, by the strength of their personalities and convictions, get other people to band together in a common cause.

That common cause might be running a Fortune 500 company, gathering donations for the local food bank or saving the environment.

The best leader might not have any title, but is the person people naturally rally behind.

A few people have an innate talent for leadership, but almost anyone can learn the skills.

Are you wondering if you have what it takes to be a great leader? Take the quiz in the Coaching Request below. How many of these qualities does it take to be a leader? My opinion? All of them. Check to see which ones

Empowering Women | Key-Dynamics.com

If you want to be a leader
act like one

deserve more effort and pledge to improve.

COACHING REQUEST

» **AUTHENTIC.** You are real. You don't change yourself, or your message, depending on who's listening.
» **PASSIONATE.** You have a deep and abiding passion, an enthusiasm that infuses others around you, bringing out the best qualities in everyone.

» **COMPASSIONATE.** You understand and interact well with others. You don't judge.

» **ACTION ORIENTED.** You work toward a measurable, defined goal – and get others to work alongside.

» **PERSISTENT.** You aren't easily sidetracked, and you don't let others wander off either. You don't give up at the first roadblock and are always looking for ways to move forward.

» **INTEGRITY.** You define your life and craft your actions to fit a personal code of honor – even if it's not convenient or makes others uncomfortable.

» **FAITH.** You believe in yourself and in your cause. You believe you're doing the right thing.

» **HONEST.** With yourself and others. You occasionally do a gut check to make sure you're on the right track, and 'fess up when you're wrong.

» **ENGAGED.** You are involved – and not just in your job-related tasks or volunteer positions, but with your colleagues and families as well.

» **ACTIVE LISTENERS.** You actually hear what people are telling you, not just waiting for them to take a breath so you can jump in with your own comments.

» **OPEN.** You know you don't have all the answers, let alone all the questions, and you're OK saying that.

» **INCLUSIVE.** You bring everyone into the tent. You don't shut out people who disagree or have different ideas.

» **RELIABLE.** You show up. You do what you say you're going to do, when you say you're going to do it. People can count on you.

» **RELEVANT.** Your actions and beliefs improve the lives of others, even in small ways. What you say and do matters.

» **FOCUSED.** You focus on what's in front of you, undistracted by ringing phones, computer emails or whoever happens to wander by.

» **HUMOROUS AND PLAYFUL.** You have a sense of humor, and that means not taking yourself too seriously. You know that play relieves stress and leads to creativity.

CHAPTER 29
HOW TO BE YOUR OWN CHEERLEADER

There's a lot of information about how to be a cheerleader for your team members, but what about those of us in management or leadership positions? How can we be our own cheerleader?

Here are some tips.

COACHING REQUEST

>> **RECOGNIZE YOUR OWN VALUE.** If you are in a leadership position, clearly someone has determined that you are worth being in charge of a project, department or team. While I don't recommend entirely basing your own feeling of self-worth on other people's opinions, it's still an important factor to keep in mind.

>> **CONNECT WITH OTHERS.** These can be men or women in your industry or those who have similar responsibilities. It's easy (particularly if you are a solopreneur) to get isolated, feeling like you're the only one in the entire galaxy who is facing specific issues or challenges. You're not. Having these connections will reassure you that you're not alone and you can get support from others who may very well have faced – and resolved – the same problems. Even better: You may have solutions to their problems.

>> **TAKE CREDIT.** Women have a horrible problem with this. They have been brought up to believe that "nice girls" don't pat themselves on the back. There is a huge difference between honestly acknowledging your role in a particular success and dashing into a room and shouting at the top of your lungs, "Look what I did! Aren't I fabulous! Yay, me!"

>> **UNDERSTAND THE DIFFERENCE BETWEEN INTERNAL AND EXTERNAL FACTORS TO SUCCESS.** Research on "imposter syndrome," dating back to the late 1970s, shows that women disproportionately believe that their success is based on things outside of themselves, and therefore liable to disappear like a puddle on a sunny day. External factors include luck, timing and even deceiving others into believing they are competent.

>> **CREATE A SUCCESS FILE.** Make a list of everything you've accomplished – objective, concrete achievements as well as the underlying, internal factors that led to those achievements. They could be determination, strong work ethic, resilience, exceptional focus, crackerjack research skills and so on. You own these qualities; no one has given them to you.

>> **KEEP A FEEDBACK FILE.** Make a note of every time you've been complimented – and how you reacted to that compliment. Accepting a compliment is hard for many women, but it can be learned. Most will reflexively say, "Thank you, but... I was lucky. I had just a small role. I'm not sure why I got the job/assignment/promotion/client." Once you're comfortable receiving compliments, you can add, "Thank you for noticing. I worked hard on that project" or "I'm proud of the results we achieved." Accepting a compliment is not the same as bragging.

Are you hiding your true self?

» **STOP BEING A PHONY.** This is a bizarre spiral that is especially problematic for us women. We have been brought up in a society that does not value our competence, so we tend to hide those qualities to avoid rejection. We will not offer differing viewpoints, and instead may tell people what they want to hear. Because we have kept our true selves under wraps, any honor or accolade will be seen as obtained under false pretenses, further eroding our belief in our own value. It erodes our trust in others, too; how much respect do they deserve from us if they were so easily deceived? Just be you. The world will not come to an end if you speak up.

» **FOCUS ON BEING *YOUR* BEST, NOT *THE* BEST.** You are not perfect. You will never be perfect. Get over it. The good news: No one else is perfect, either. Do the best you can, learn and grow, but stop comparing yourself to others. Comparison is the death of joy.

» **WHAT WOULD YOUR COACH SAY?** Step back and look at your situation from a more objective but still supportive point of view. When you feel downtrodden, imagine what your coach would say. I know what I would say: "Is this really true or a story you're telling yourself?"

CHAPTER 30

YOUR SUCCESS MECHANISM

More than 50 years ago, plastic surgeon Maxwell Maltz made a remarkable discovery: Some of his patients — after radical surgery to improve their appearance — still felt ugly.

Some of them went so far as to deny that any cosmetic surgery had been done at all... despite "before and after" photos that clearly showed the difference.

That led Maltz to explore the world of self-image and its impact on us in our everyday lives.

He looked to the then-new discipline of cybernetics, "the science of communications and automatic control systems in both machines and living things," to explain the impact of self-image and how to change it.

Maltz concluded that our subconscious mind is an impersonal, automatic, goal-striving machine that achieves what our conscious mind tells it to do.

Just like a guided missile gets feedback from radar, sonar and other "sense organs" to stay on target, so does the center fielder use feedback from the speed of the ball, wind direction and so forth to reach his target – catching a fly ball.

In a similar fashion, the "servo-mechanism" of our subconscious takes the feedback we give it through our thoughts, words and deeds to help us reach our own target.

The Law of Attraction before there was a Law of Attraction!

In order to succeed, Maltz believed that we must have a Success Mechanism — a target or goal — and use our imagination to envision it.

In his book, Maltz gave many examples of how imagination helps people reach their goals. He wrote about the chess player who toppled a world champion by spending three months playing chess only in his mind. He recounted the story of a concert pianist who practiced mostly in his own head.

Napoleon "practiced" soldiering for many years before taking to the battlefield. Conrad Hilton played hotel operator as a boy.

What **LIES** are you telling **yourself?**

And in the years since *Psycho-Cybernetics* was published, we've seen many world-class athletes do the same type thing with extraordinary results: They imagine every step, every feeling, every sense, as if they were real, all the way to the winner's circle.

We all have our own examples, even if it's something as simple as imagining a wad of paper hitting the center of wastebasket... and then dunking it.

Our imaginations are powerful. A person walking in the woods, suddenly confronted by an actor in a realistic bear costume, will have the same physiological reaction as if confronted by a real bear.

Truth is not the issue — it's what you think that matters.

And so we come to our own Success Mechanism: If you think you are stupid, ugly, shy, fat, weak, inferior or poor, you are. Your image of yourself has become your reality.

If you've got negative images of yourself that are driving your reality, it's time to use your rational brain to examine and re-evaluate these beliefs.

What kind of feedback are you providing your own "servo-mechanism" to reach your target? Ask yourself the questions that follow. Use the answers to reconfigure your own "servo-mechanism" and prime your Success Mechanism by imagining what you want... in all its glorious, Technicolor detail.

COACHING REQUEST

» Why do I believe this?
» Is this actually true or something I've assumed or something someone told me years ago?
» Is it possible that I'm mistaken?
» If this isn't true, why should I keep acting and feeling as if it were?
» If I were looking at someone else in the same situation, would I think the same thing?

CHAPTER 31
HOW FEAR HOLDS US BACK

Fear and excitement are the opposite sides of the **same coin**

We all want to be successful, right? So what's stopping us?

Fear. Fear of failure, sure, but fear of success as well. The first is easy to understand (although it can be embarrassing to admit it to ourselves), but the latter has always puzzled me.

Why in the world would we be afraid to succeed?

Fear holds us back from success because we are hard-wired to survive. If we take that chance – make that big change – in order to succeed, that threatens our survival, at least to our lizard-brain.

We may not be happy with where we are, but you know what? It's safe. It's comfortable (even when it isn't – the devil you know, after all). It's what we know.

What keeps us "safe" from failure, unfortunately, also keeps us from success.

Our lizard-brain doesn't know the difference between keeping us physically safe and psychologically safe. To that part of us, anything that upsets the status quo is a threat. Changing jobs, ending bad relationships, moving to that place where we always dreamed of living – these are all risks. And any risk is a threat, which is a menace to our self-preservation.

So there we are. Stuck. Making the same excuses, letting our lizard-brain govern our conscious lives, keeping us small and preventing us from exercising our desire to do more and better.

If you have a fear of something that interferes with the activities of daily living, like the fear of being outside, please seek qualified professional help.

But if the things you fear are not life-threatening and keep you from becoming the highest and best "you" that you can be, answer the questions below.

COACHING REQUEST

>> **WHAT AM I AFRAID OF?** What, specifically, holds you back? Keep asking yourself "why" until you get to the cause of your fear.
>> **IS IT REALISTIC?** Will doing what you fear put you in physical danger? Is what you fear likely to occur? Assign a percentage to it.

» **WHAT NEEDS TO CHANGE?** Many times, what we fear is simply based on a lack of knowledge, the proverbial "fear of the unknown." That's easy enough to resolve. What can you do to learn more? Who can you ask about it? Use your rational mind instead of letting your lizard-brain control your life.

» **WHAT'S THE VERY WORST THING THAT CAN HAPPEN?** Take it to the extreme. Then ask yourself: If the worst thing does happen, can I survive it? Most of our fears involve the ego – being embarrassed or looking foolish or having people laugh at us. All of those are survivable; very few of the things we fear are fatal.

For an action plan on how to overcome those fears, use the above information as your baseline and please see the workbook.

CHAPTER 32

GETTING SMART

What's preventing you from being more effective with your time management?

be a goal digger

Most people in my Facebook time management group are suffering from distractions and resultant lack of focus. This is so easy to do if you spend a lot of time on the Internet, especially if you have to be online for business.

Or you get up for that cup of coffee, or a potty break, and pretty soon you're dusting tables, picking up stray papers, watering plants and schmoozing with the guy in the next cubby.

If you want to be more efficient, you have to set time management goals. The best ones are SMART goals – specific, measurable, attainable, realistic and time-bound. This method of creating goals works well in every area of your life, not just in time management.

How can you get a grip on your time in a SMART way?

COACHING REQUEST

SET YOUR SMART GOALS:

>> **SPECIFIC.** What exactly is it you want to accomplish with time management? Let's use "reduce distractions." The next step is to make it...

>> **MEASURABLE.** How will you quantify this goal? "I will limit my web surfing to three times a day" is one possibility. What are others?

>> **ATTAINABLE.** This is your first gut check. Can you shut down the browser for most of the day? The answer to this is probably yes, but is it...

>> **REALISTIC.** The answer to this also is probably yes, even if your job is to be online 100% of the day. Focusing on work projects is one thing; checking your Twitter feed 20 times a day or cruising through funny memes on Facebook every half hour is something else entirely. Time to go back to **MEASURABLE** and add in some quantifiers.

>> **TIME-BOUND.** This is your end date or your start time, whichever fits best with your goal. It could be "starting right this minute" or "by this date."

>> **FINAL SMART GOAL.** After tweaking, this time management goal might read something like this: "Starting today, I will reduce my distractions by limiting my personal web surfing to three times a day, 10 minutes each. To keep on track, I will set a timer and stop when 10 minutes is up."

CHAPTER 33
HOW TO FINISH WHAT YOU START

DO YOU PUT THINGS OFF, OVER AND OVER AGAIN? TAKE THIS QUIZ TO SEE IF YOU'RE A MASTER PROCRASTINATOR.

» You miss opportunities to buy tickets for concerts, sporting events and other activities.

» You get penalized for paying your bills late.

» Your gift cards expire before you can use them.

» You wait until Christmas Eve to buy gifts.

» You drink more alcohol than you intend.

» You lie to yourself, as in "I'll do this tomorrow" or "I work best with a deadline" or "I'm more creative when I'm under pressure." (I've heard them all, believe me!)

» You squander your resources.

» You actively look for distractions, like checking email or surfing the web.

» You get a rush from waiting till the last minute.

» Deep down, you fear you'll fail – so why even start?

» You can't decide.

» You get more colds than your friends, you don't sleep well and your gut is in turmoil.

If you answered yes to nearly all these questions – and about 20% fall into the category of "chronic procrastinator" – you need more support than you'll get from this chapter. Find a professional therapist who can help you sort through your underlying issues.

However, if you're in the other 80% who merely puts things off from time to time, read on. There are things you can do to help with procrastination and improve your ability to accomplish what you want in a timely fashion.

COACHING REQUEST

» **UNCOVER YOUR "WHY."** More than anything else, this is what will help you stay on track. What you're trying to learn is *how you will feel* when you reach your goal. Keep asking the question until you get the answer.

» **DON'T MULTITASK.** Research has shown that when you try to do multiple things at once, your functional IQ drops by 10 points – more than if you smoked marijuana. Finish each task before you move on to the next.

» **MAKE A TO-DO LIST AND PRIORITIZE IT.** Do the most important first, the second most important next and so on. For a great way to organize your time, see "How to Use a Planner" in the workbook.

>> **BREAK BIGS INTO LITTLES.** One thing that contributes to feeling overwhelmed – which leads to procrastination – is that we cut off too big a chunk. Turn the big task into a series of little ones, and celebrate as you finish them.

>> **DELEGATE.** You don't have to do everything yourself. Honest. Delegate those things that others can do better, and focus on those things that only you can do. Don't kid yourself that only you can do things the right way.

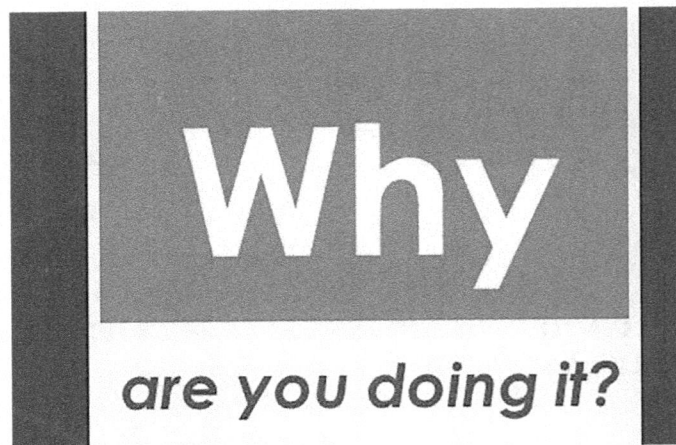

Why are you doing it?

>> **YOU HAVE A CHOICE.** Beware of the "should" in your life. Some are unavoidable (such as "I should pay the electric bill"). Others you bring on yourself, such as "I should be a better employee and help John finish his work." You get to choose.

>> **DECLUTTER.** A messy office or home leads to inefficiency. That will make you lose time, too – an estimated hour a day. That's a lot of time that you could be doing something worthwhile – like having fun!

>> **BEGIN.** Don't focus on the end; focus on the beginning. Just begin! You can massage and improve and polish later.

>> **GO EASY ON YOURSELF.** Perfectionism is the handmaiden of procrastination. If you put too much pressure on yourself to do the job perfectly, you're much more likely to put it off.

>> **SCHEDULE BREAKS.** If you think something is going to take hours and hours to complete, make sure you schedule in some time away from the project. (Efficiency experts say you should take a break every 50 to 90 minutes.) You'll be much less likely to procrastinate and you'll be more refreshed. And who knows? You may have a stellar idea that occurs to you while you're walking around the block.

>> **WATCH YOUR SELF-TALK.** We often talk ourselves into procrastination. Instead of saying, "I don't feel like doing this right now" or "There's too much work here!" say instead, "Even if I can't get the whole thing done, I can get started on this part."

CHAPTER 34

DEALING WITH GOSSIP

> He who gossips to you will gossip about you.

People gossip for many reasons. They could be trying to ingratiate themselves. They could be frustrated, angry, anxious or bored.

Whatever the motivation, gossip is hurtful and unproductive — a 2002 study says an average of 65 hours per person is frittered away each year in office gossip. Gossip breeds mistrust, self-esteem and self-confidence issues, lots of anxiety and low morale.

Stopping gossip starts with you, the boss.

COACHING REQUEST

» **LEAD BY EXAMPLE.** Don't participate in gossip; that just gives others the green light to do it.

» **IMPROVE YOUR COMMUNICATIONS.** Meet with your entire staff at least once a month to pass along important information; always check for understanding before moving on to the next topic or task. Communicate regularly outside of formal meetings. Let your colleagues know you're available to answer their questions. If you can't meet face-to-face, it's OK to put it in writing – but do so cautiously. Written communications are easily misunderstood. Try a weekly email to fill in the gaps between group meetings.

» **CONSIDER A FIVE-MINUTE "GOSSIP" BREAK.** Before you start your meeting, let people share what they've heard and use that opportunity to give people the facts. The more information you share with your staff, the less need there will be to gossip.

» **TALK ABOUT GOSSIP.** If your shop has a problem with gossip, talk about the issue and establish the standard: Gossip will not be tolerated. Tackle it as a group issue, because to change the culture, everyone is going to have to buy in.

» **DEAL WITH INVETERATE GOSSIPS INDIVIDUALLY.** Tolerance begets more gossip.

» **THREE WAYS TO DEAL WITH GOSSIP ABOUT OTHERS.** You can walk away, change the subject or use these gossip-stoppers:

  ○ "I'm not comfortable talking about ___."
  ○ "I don't like talking about other people because I don't want them talking about me."
  ○ "Have you told Jane that directly?"
  ○ "If this really bothers you, you should go talk to him about it, not to me."
  ○ "Really? I've always found her to be ___. Do you know if your information is correct?"
  ○ "Let's hold off on talking about Anne until she's here." And my personal favorite:
  ○ "I hadn't heard that about ___. Let's go ask him!"

» **MEET GOSSIP ABOUT YOU HEAD-ON.** Go to the gossiper and say: "I heard that you've been saying XX about me. Please come to me directly with any questions or comments rather than talking with others about it."

CHAPTER 35
DEALING WITH PASSIVE-AGGRESSIVES

Do you work with someone who is passive-aggressive? It used to be called being "two-faced" or "back-stabbing" – agreeable to your face and something else entirely when you weren't around.

Whatever term you use, it's one of four basic approaches to life:

1. **ASSERTIVENESS.** You stand up for your rights without violating the rights of others. It's about tactfully but plainly saying what you want, without feeling guilty.
2. **AGGRESSIVENESS.** In-your-face confrontation, doing whatever it takes to win. The aggressive person doesn't care about what you want or need. All he wants is what he wants and he's going to go for it, regardless of the cost to you and others.
3. **PASSIVITY.** Often manifests itself as weak, compliant and self-sacrificing. Goes along with everyone. About everything.
4. **PASSIVE-AGGRESSIVE.** Blames others for their own shortcomings, takes credit for work someone else has performed and argues about unimportant matters.

Most passive-aggressive personalities appear charming, rarely demonstrate anger and are almost always agreeable. Unfortunately, there is a big disconnect between how they appear and how they behave.

They hide their annoyance, impatience or resentment behind a calm and happy façade. They may also be master procrastinators, and pretend to not see, hear, remember or understand requests.

A passive-aggressive person will often give you the silent treatment, becoming sulky and withdrawn. And they love to gossip as a way to express their anger and hostility.

Here are some ways to deal with passive-aggressives.

COACHING REQUEST

>> **RECOGNIZE THE BEHAVIOR.** This is the first step in knowing how to deal with it.
>> **CONFRONT IT.** Passive-aggressive individuals avoid directly expressing their feelings or acknowledging their anger. In a non-judgmental way, tell him, "This conversation seems to be making you angry" or "I get the feeling that you're upset by this."
>> **EXPECT DENIAL, AND ACCEPT IT.** When the other person denies it, don't argue. You won't win. Instead, say, "All right. I just wanted to let you know how it appears to me."
>> **KEEP CALM.** Getting under your skin gives passive-aggressives a rush. They love it when you get hurt, angry or go on the attack. Keep your head and you'll feel more in control of the situation and yourself. Plus, you'll deny them the satisfaction they crave.

» **DEMAND HONESTY.** If you feel you're being lied to, call him on it calmly. Don't get sidetracked into alleys that will turn into a verbal fistfight of "he said/she said."

» **DEFEND OTHERS.** Don't be afraid to stick up for other people who face a passive-aggressive's gossip or personal attacks. Tell him, "I don't listen to gossip" and walk away.

» **BE FRIENDLY, BUT AVOID GETTING TOO PERSONAL.** A passive-aggressive coworker will use what you say to talk about you behind your back.

» **TAKE NOTES.** Write down all important information from the conversation. If anything goes wrong, a passive-aggressive coworker will throw you from the bridge. Be sure you have something in writing to support your position.

» **TALK WITH YOUR SUPERVISOR, IF YOU HAVE ONE.** Remember, passive-aggressive people love to pass the buck, and they will try to dump their errors in your lap. Let your supervisor know about your co-worker's behavior and performance.

» **WATCH YOUR LANGUAGE!** One of the worst things you can do is tell your boss that your colleague is a lazy, shiftless, SOB... even if he is.

» **DESCRIBE THE ACTIONS AND BEHAVIORS.** Let your boss come to her own conclusions. Say, "She missed five deadlines" or "He has asked me 10 times to explain this task." Be sure you have all these documented.

CHAPTER 36
WORK-LIFE BALANCE

About a hundred years ago, starry-eyed optimists gazed into the future and saw technology taking over the mundane tasks of daily living – and working – leaving humanity with much more time for leisure.

It hasn't quite worked out that way.

Between 1977 and 1997, full-time employees in the United States increased their weekly average of hours worked by 3.5 hours – to a total to 47.1 hours.

Most Americans average 10 vacation days a year, compared to 25 days in Great Britain and 30 days in Germany. And 25% of U.S. workers take no holidays at all. Americans work a full 12 weeks more per year than Europeans.

That wonderful technology that would free us from drudgery? It's had the opposite effect, allowing many corporations to downsize their workforce and creating a much heavier workload for those who are left.

The bottom line: Family, home, community, relationships and health suffer.

In a 2000 study of United Kingdom workplace managers, 65% said work was damaging their health and 77% admitted that it affected their relationship with their children.

Based on diaries completed by 21,000 British couples, the Office of National Statistics found that the average British couple spends just 15 minutes a day enjoying a social life.

Macy's, which employs 30,000 people, came to the conclusion that an employee's personal life also affects the quality of their work on the job.

A recent survey of 300 jobseekers conducted for the New York Times showed that 75% of people looking for a new job were doing so because of the stress in their current workplace.

Some companies have stepped forward with programs to help cope with work-life balance, a phrase that first appeared in our vernacular some 20 years ago.

Flex time, flex space, flex careers, flex leaves, job sharing, on-site day care, in-house holistic therapies such as Reiki and massage, and even concierge services – hiring someone to go out and do all those errands that eat into staffers' free time – have all been tried.

They do work... when they are implemented. But not all companies have the top management's commitment or the wherewithal to offer such opportunities.

If your company offers none of these options, answering the questions in the following Coaching Request can help you create your own work-life balance.

COACHING REQUEST

» What am I doing to take care of myself?

» What three areas of my life are giving me the most stress and what will I do to eliminate them altogether? (Yes, it can be done.)

» Who or what in my work and home environment depletes my energy? How can I change that?

» What 10 things give me enormous pleasure? How can I do more of those things? Tip: If you have to schedule these things as "appointments" with yourself, do it!

» What more can I do to take care of my physical, emotional, mental and spiritual health?

» Who are five people that I can turn to for support?

» What 10 things (people, beliefs, ideas, etc.) do I need to release to get the most enjoyment out of my life?

CHAPTER 37

SHARING THE HOUSEHOLD LOAD

Here's a shocker: Household work disproportionately falls on women.

The American Time Use Survey, done by the U.S. Bureau of Labor Statistics and released in 2014, found that men do about 31% of all household work.

That means the other 69% is being done by the woman of the house, even if she stays at home, works from home or toils in an office elsewhere.

Consider also that women are generally the caregivers, not just of their own kids, if they have them, but aged parents, too. Caregiver.org stated:

>> An estimated 66% of caregivers are female.
>> The average caregiver is a 49-year-old woman, caring for her mother, who does not live with her. She is married and employed.
>> Although men also provide assistance, female caregivers may spend as much as 50% more time providing care than male caregivers.

How many hours do they work?

>> A stay-at-home mom works about 96 hours, according to Salary.com.
>> Entrepreneurs, on average, work 60 hours a week.
>> Work-at-home moms work on their business after they've taken care of the family and household chores. Depending on their energy levels, that can – and often does – extend deep into the night.
>> The average American employee works 47 hours a week. If this woman spends another 2.5 hours a day cooking, cleaning, laundry, caring for others and so on, you're looking at a workweek that is approaching 65 hours.

Whew! Is it any wonder women are exhausted all the time?

What follows is for those of you who need help getting your partner off their butt.

COACHING REQUEST

>> *KEEP TRACK OF YOUR TIME* for a week, broken down into 15-minute increments. (My handy-dandy time log is included in the workbook).
>> *ANALYZE THE DATA.* How much time is spent in food preparation, laundry, house cleaning, childcare, trips to the doctor/store, taking out the garbage, etc.? Prepare a list with the aggregated data.
>> *CREATE A LIST OF JOB DUTIES THAT MUST BE DONE EVERY WEEK.* Use the daily time log in the workbook as a baseline.

» **ADD YOUR PARTNER'S CONTRIBUTIONS** to the list.

» **CALL A FAMILY MEETING.** If you've got kids old enough to walk, include them, too. Even a 2-year-old can and should be taught to pick up toys, clothes, etc. It's the parents' job to eventually release their children into the wild with enough skills to be able to survive on their own.

» **SHOW THE FAMILY THE LIST.** It should include all that has to be done each week. Ask each family member, one at a time, what tasks they would like to take on. This makes it something they want to do, as opposed to what they are forced to do. Tell them that when all the fun things have been taken, they'll also have to sign up for some unsavory duties. If you can make a game out of it — young kids are always up for games — so much the better.

» **SPLIT THE "BIG PEOPLE'S" LIST** – the driving, cooking, cleaning, lawn care and so on. There are some things that you may have to do by default, like taking care of the kids if you do not hold a job outside the house. Keep that in mind as the rest of the tasks are meted out.

» **REVISIT THE LIST ONCE A MONTH.** Do this as a family to see if the duties need to be shuffled. It's especially important if there is a lot of competition for one task. No one wants to get stuck taking out the garbage until they're ready for college. Plus, as the kids get older, they'll improve their skill level and can handle bigger responsibilities. You may offer a sweetener — say, a small weekly stipend or a monthly family trip to the zoo. This is completely optional, as children need to understand that some things just have to be done, with or without a reward. Life is like that.

» **OUTSOURCE.** Before you automatically say you can't afford it, consider this: If you make more money per hour than you would pay someone else to do the task, consider hiring it out. This is also a quality-of-life issue as well. You need "me" time, even if it's just sprawling out on the couch and reading a good book.

CHAPTER 38
YOU HAVE THE RIGHT TO YOUR OWN FEELINGS

A woman I know told me about a situation with one of her vendors.

"Up until recently I thought I had a pretty good relationship with one of my vendors. But not too long ago. I was in a group demonstration, joshing around, when out of the blue, the vendor made an insulting personal comment about me.

"I was shocked and felt humiliated in front of my peers. I pretended it didn't bother me, but it did. Honestly, I can't remember what preceded the exchange. Maybe I started it. But the more I think about it, the angrier I feel.

"What should I do? Complain to the boss? Find another vendor? Pretend it didn't happen?"

The short answer I gave her – and would give to anyone else in her situation – is you need to clear the air if you intend to deal with this person in the future.

And the sooner you do it, the better you will feel.

You need to lay out your feelings, always a scary thought, but in the end you'll be relieved to get it off your chest and feel great about your ability to stick up for yourself.

You can do this! It comes down to technique and practice.

COACHING REQUEST

>> **WRITE DOWN WHAT YOU FEEL.** Humiliation, shock and anger – what else?

>> **WRITE A SPEECH.** Focus on how you felt. Let it all hang out, baby!

>> **REWRITE THE SPEECH.** Go back and cut out all the accusations, old arguments and slurs about the offender's heritage, IQ, sexual habits, appearance and so on.

>> **KNOW YOUR BOTTOM LINE.** What do you want? What will you do if you don't get it?

>> **SET THE STAGE.** Say something like: "I've really liked working with you over the last few years. Your product is good and our customers like it. However, you said some things at the demonstration that really bothered me."

>> **OWN UP TO YOUR OWN FEELINGS.** Move on to: "When you said X, I felt humiliated/embarrassed/etc., in front of my colleagues. Now I'm angry, too. I like you and your product, but I'm not sure I can work with you any longer."

>> **IDENTIFY WHAT YOU WANT.** Wrap it up with "I need to know that you will never to speak to me that way again." Or "I want to be treated professionally and courteously in the future. Can you assure me of that?"

>> **WHAT'S THE WORST THAT CAN HAPPEN?** Do you think the other person will cry? Accuse you of

unspeakable acts? Cuss you out? Throw objects? Practice those worst-case scenarios with someone who knows assertiveness techniques that can help you calmly meet any situation and still stay on target.

» **PRACTICE YOUR SPEECH OUT LOUD.** I recommend a coach who can help you spot pseudo-feelings, such as, "I feel you're an idiot or you wouldn't have said such a stupid thing," but if you have a trusted other who can help you stay on track, that works, too.

» **REPEAT.** Keep going over it until you can deliver your message calmly, without fumbling, breaking down or getting distracted.

» **SET UP A TIME TO TALK.** You can do it in person or over the phone. You may want to pick a public place, with a private space, to minimize emotional reactions – yours and the other person's. But please – no emails!

» **DELIVER YOUR SPEECH.**

» **SHUT UP AND LISTEN.** Let the other person respond. I predict with 95% certainty that this issue will be resolved with an apology. If you don't get what you want, take your pre-determined action.

CHAPTER 39
RELEASING YOUR INNER CONTROL FREAK

Do you demand perfection from yourself and others?

How's that working out for you?

Perfection is unattainable and being a control freak will hurt you, personally and professionally.

Because you cannot be perfect, you will beat yourself up, your stress levels will soar and probably your blood pressure along with it.

Being a perfectionist and a control freak means, at the very least, you'll end up doing other people's work for them, or solve all their problems all the time. At worst, you will work longer hours to get your own stuff done, neglect your duties and/or destroy your own career path because you cannot manage yourself or others.

If the idea of relying on other people to "do things right" – meaning your way – makes you feel like Life as We Know It is about to end, this is for you.

If you want to stop doing everything yourself and simply don't have the tools to know how to do it, go to the next chapter. For now, complete the Coaching Request below to get a better handle on your inner control freak.

COACHING REQUEST

>> *LOOK AT YOUR BEHAVIOR.* Do you insist on telling people how to do their tasks? Do you complain (at least mentally) when the job isn't done the way you would do it? Do you redo work that has already completed by someone else because it doesn't meet your personal standards?

>> *LOOK AT YOUR BIG PICTURE.* What do you gain by this behavior? (You always gain something; otherwise, you wouldn't to it.) What do you lose? How does this impact your health and your performance?

>> *LOOK AT THE COMPANY'S BIG PICTURE.* What does your company gain? Lose? How does your behavior affect employee retention and productivity? Do your employees feel valued and heard?

CHAPTER 40

HOW TO STOP DOING IT ALL YOURSELF

Praise is a great tool to create the behavior you want to see as well as a way to reinforce good behavior you do see.

Let's look at the employee who couldn't solve a problem if his life depended on it.

Jonathon has the annoying tendency to bring the entire office to a screeching halt every time something unusual happens – which appears to be virtually everything – and doesn't know how to handle it.

You, of course, being the stellar manager (and closet control freak) that you are, can troubleshoot most problems without breaking a sweat and you rush to his aid. The first time. The second time.

The hundredth time. And endlessly into the future because you're handling it so well.

I predict this is affecting your health and probably even your job performance, because when you're solving other people's problems, when do you get the chance to do your own stuff?

It's time to learn how to delegate before you run yourself into the ground. With the right nurturing, chances are excellent that you can turn your biggest pain in the butt into your company's top problem-solver.

COACHING REQUEST

» **STOP SOLVING THE PROBLEM FOR HIM.** Say, "Gosh, Jonathon, you're right! That really is mind-boggling. What do YOU think we should do?"

» **WHEN HE SAYS "I DON'T KNOW" – AND YOU KNOW HE WILL.** "Well, if you knew the answer, what would it be?" Ninety-nine times out of 100, Jonathon will come up with an answer. All he needs is the permission to express it.

» **DIG DEEPER.** Say something like "That's an interesting approach. What else?" This is especially helpful if his solution sounds dubious. Keep repeating the "what else" step until Jonathon is dry of ideas.

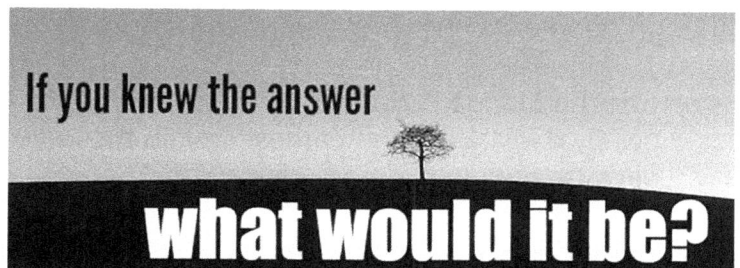
If you knew the answer what would it be?

» **ASK HIM THE PROS AND CONS OF EACH SUGGESTION.** Ask him which of his ideas seems to be the best solution. If no small children will die as a result and it won't bankrupt the company, let him carry through his best idea.

» **KEEP TABS ON HIM.** Ask him how it's going. See if he needs anything more to solve the problem. Let him do it. And praise him abundantly for getting it done – even if it isn't exactly the way you would do it.

CHAPTER 41
ART OF THE HANDSHAKE

One of the things that just tickles me is showing girls as young as 5 how to shake hands. I solemnly tell them that it's important for a woman to have a strong handshake so they will be taken seriously and treated with respect.

Not only do they love it, but it takes, on average, about three shakes to perfect their technique.

Based on my experience at a recent networking gathering, I may need to branch out to show the Secrets of the Handshake to adult women, too.

One woman took my hand in hers and gave it exactly two shoulder-wrenching pumps, like she was trying to get the last molecule of water out of a dying well.

No doubt you've also experienced the Pump Handle as well as the You-Old-Cuss Arm Waggle, the Dead Fish Shake, the I-Work-Out Crusher Grip, the Long-Time-No-See Shake and Back Thump, the I'm-Really-Sincere Double-Handshake and many more.

The Arm Waggle starts out as a Standard Handshake (more or that later), and then turns into a swinging hammock between your two bodies, moving the arm vigorously side to side from the shoulder. Woe betide you if you've got rotator cuff issues.

The Double-Handshake is the favorite of politicians, although people in other professions use it, too.

The Shake and Thump

It starts as the Standard Handshake, then they place their other hand over yours for extra impact. And you just know, by the sincere and earnest look in their eyes, that if they had a third hand, it also would come into play – because they really, really care.

A variant on this is the Upper Arm Rest. First comes the Standard Handshake, then the other hand migrates to your upper arm, which is either squeezed, patted or lightly punched, depending on the circumstances and gender of the recipient.

The Shake and Thump is mostly a guy thing, particularly between men who have deep affection for each other but don't want onlookers to think they are sleeping together.

I have employed it myself, usually when I'm going in for hug and he's got his hand stuck out, so we strike something of an compromise: I shake his hand, and stretch my awkwardly suspended hugging arm around his back for a couple of quick, gruff guy thumps.

SOME THINGS YOU SHOULD NEVER DO:

» *FORCE A STANDARD HANDSHAKE ON ANYONE.* If a woman offers you a limp hand, go with it. She probably is Very Old School or is a member of some royal family.

» *OFFER THE DEAD FISH.* For some reason, many men (and even some women) think that women are delicate flowers – or high-earning concert pianists – who can only use their fingertips while shaking hands. Their fingers touch yours in a way that makes it seem that they fear you'll give them cooties.

» *THE CRUSHER GRIP.* I have never had a woman do this to me, but some men like to use this knuckle-grinding grip as a way to show that they have way more testosterone than you do. Fine. They can keep it.

So what is the Standard Handshake? Read on!

COACHING REQUEST

» *GRASP THE OTHER PERSON'S HAND*, palm to palm, your thumb firmly seated against his. Give his hand two or three moderate shakes and boom! You're done.

» *PRACTICE.* Beginners always have a bit of an issue with the right amount of squeeze to apply, so ask for feedback from your practice partner. If young girls can get it right quickly, it should be just as easy for adults – as long as you don't have to unlearn bad habits.

» *FEEL FREE TO MODIFY.* It can be changed according to circumstances and affection level.

CHAPTER 42
NETWORKING FOR INTROVERTS

She's new to the area and wants to meet people, so she joins one of the local organizations.

The problem is, she has no idea what to do after she shows up for her first gathering.

So there she stands, drink in one hand, plate of munchies in the other, and people flow around her as if she were a pothole in the road.

Meeting new people – whether for personal or business reasons – can be nerve-wracking, especially for the shy or introverted.

Networking tip:
Mix and mingle

Everyone knows networking is important, but no one teaches you how to do it.

Here are some easy tips that may make it easier.

COACHING REQUEST

>> *WALK IN WITH A SMILE.* Make sure your body language is open and welcoming. No hunched shoulders, no arms crossed over your chest.

>> *MAKE EYE CONTACT.*

>> *SAY SOMETHING.* It doesn't have to be profound; pick up something from the environment: "Wow, what a great turnout" or "This buffet looks great." Offer a sincere compliment: "Those are absolutely killer shoes you're wearing" or "Terrific tie."

>> *INTRODUCE YOURSELF AND OFFER A HANDSHAKE.* Unless, of course, the other person has both hands full. Keep one of your hands free, too. Make sure your handshake is firm – wimpy handshakes are worse than day-old fish. (See Art of the Handshake for details)

>> *ADD A BIT OF INFORMATION ABOUT YOURSELF.* Maybe it's as basic as "I'm new here" or "I just started at XYZ." Or you could say something a little more revealing, like "Crowds make me nervous. I hope I don't spill my drink!" Don't put yourself down, but showing your human side may put the other person at ease, too.

>> *ASK OPEN-ENDED QUESTIONS.* People love talking about themselves and generally, all you have to do is nod and make appropriate noises at the right time to keep it moving along. Here are some samples.

1. *"HOW DID YOU GET INTO YOUR CURRENT JOB?"* The answer to this question is likely to reveal a great number of things about your companion and help you connect on a personal level. Feel free to point out any similarities between you without making the conversation about you.

2. **"WHAT DO YOU ENJOY MOST ABOUT YOUR JOB?"** You can settle for the short version – "I love meeting people" – or you can drill down by following up with, "What is it you enjoy most about that?"

» **KEEP MOVING.** Tell your fellow traveler how much you've enjoyed your talk, that you don't want to monopolize his time, and how welcome he's made you feel. If appropriate, exchange business cards or other contact information, and tell him you'd like to be in touch.

> *Special tip: As soon as you can after collecting the cards, jot a note on the back detailing where you met these people and any distinguishing characteristics- from Ohio, has 12 kids, loves to ski, etc.*

» **FOLLOW UP** as soon as you can after the meeting. I recommend sending an email that says it was pleasure to meet him and that you look forward to the next time. Add to your message, depending on what you talked about when you met. It will flatter them to know they made an impression.

CHAPTER 43
THE BEST WAY TO IMPROVE YOUR SELF-CONFIDENCE

Do you suffer from glossophobia? Relax! It's not going to kill you. Plenty of people – a whopping 74% – are terrified of public speaking.

Improving your public speaking skills is one of the best ways to boost your self-confidence. You'll be more comfortable at networking events, you won't freeze when asked to introduce yourself to a group and you'll be able to speak your mind on issues that are important to you.

The key to overcoming your fear of public speaking is to be prepared. As with any learned skill, the more you practice, the easier it will get. It won't be long before you look forward to speaking in front of crowds. Promise!

Complete this Coaching Request to get started.

COACHING REQUEST

» **PREPARE YOUR SPEECH.** Write it down. Don't worry about structure, grammar, spelling, punctuation or anything else at this stage; just write it down.

» **ORGANIZE IT.** Make sure it covers all your main points. Tie the end to the beginning, if possible.

» **ADD HUMOR.** A joke at the beginning of your speech will get people laughing and set a relaxing tone. Be sure your humor is appropriate for the crowd and the occasion. One of my favorite icebreakers: "When I asked how long I could speak, I was told, 'Take as long as you like, but we're leaving in 20 minutes.'"

» **PRACTICE, PRACTICE, PRACTICE.** Read your speech aloud. Over and over and over again. You need to hear what you're saying. Consider recording your speech.

» **WATCH YOUR AHS AND UMS:** It's better to say nothing than use these annoying filler sounds.

» **SMOOTH OUT THE ROUGH SPOTS.** Every time you stumble, you need to polish. Remember, your goal is to make it sound like you're talking to friends.

» **BUILD IN PAUSES.** Well-timed pauses, built into your speech, are excellent public-speaking techniques. Even a few seconds of silence will capture your audience's attention and emphasize what comes next.

» **TIME YOURSELF.** Adjust your content according to how much time you've been given. If there is a Q&A after your speech, be sure to allow for that.

» **DON'T MEMORIZE YOUR SPEECH.** It keeps you from being present, gauging your audience's reactions and responding to them. Plus, if your mind suddenly goes blank, you're screwed. Take your notes, stapled together for security, to the podium or microphone.

» **DO NOT READ YOUR SPEECH WORD FOR WORD FROM YOUR NOTES!** When you're at the podium, use a finger to keep your place in your speech in case you need to glance down to remind yourself of what comes next. If you have no podium, hold your notes in your hand and keep track with your thumb. Some people use file cards instead of regular paper. Use your best judgment. That's fine for short speeches, but if you're holding 30 or more cards, what would happen if they slipped from your hands?

» **TAKE A BATHROOM BREAK.** Once you arrive at the venue, make sure you don't have food lodged in your teeth. If you wear makeup, give it a last check. Is everything properly fastened? Is your skirt tucked into your pantyhose?

» **RELAX.** Take a few deep breaths. A certain amount of tension is natural and good; it keeps you sharp.

» **THE AUDIENCE IS NOT YOUR ENEMY.** People want you to succeed. They want to hear what you have to say; otherwise, you wouldn't be there.

» **DON'T APOLOGIZE.** If you stumble, don't apologize. Don't tell people how nervous you are. Most people won't even notice.

» **EYE CONTACT.** Pick a person on the left, right and middle who looks engaged and friendly. Speak directly to these people, moving your eyes back and forth across the audience throughout your speech. It will appear that you are making eye contact with the entire group.

» **SOUND CHECK.** If you're using a microphone, keep it a few inches from your mouth. As you move your head to make eye contact, move the microphone with your mouth. (So many people forget this!) If the microphone is stationary, shift your body – but not your head – for consistent sound levels.

CHAPTER 44

SEXUAL HARASSMENT ON THE JOB

There you are, struggling to improve your revenue and keep a handle on your expenses.

You wonder how many of your employees will show up today, how you're going to pay the higher insurance premiums, hoping business improves, drowning in bureaucratic regulations.

Despite all that, you didn't realize that you were having a pretty good day – until one of your employees tells you a co-worker has been "accidentally" brushing up against her breasts every time they pass each other.

Now what?

You've already done everything you can to let your people know that sexual harassment, of either gender, will not be tolerated.

You've had the training; your staff knows sexual harassment doesn't consist only of unwanted physical contact, but could occur even with no physical contact at all. They know to be aware of improper sexual advances from vendors and clients, too.

And it doesn't even have to happen to them directly; anyone who witnesses these behaviors and considers them a "hostile working environment" is within his or her rights to file a harassment charge.

You have a written policy and you've even conducted an annual survey of your employees, asking if they feel they have experienced any sexual harassment on the job.

All should be right in your world, at least on this topic.

And now this.

Your company is too small to have a human resources department to fall back on and the heat is starting to build.

What do you do?

COACHING REQUEST

» **TAKE IMMEDIATE ACTION.** If you are not the boss, tell him or her immediately. The company can be held liable for sexual harassment even if the owners didn't know anything was going on.
» **KEEP ALL SEXUAL HARASSMENT CHARGES CONFIDENTIAL.** This protects the accused, should the allegations be false, and the accuser, should they be true.
» **IF YOU ARE THE BOSS, TALK TO LEGAL COUNSEL.** It's always good to have a licensed professional

covering your back. A little hand-holding can be wonderfully comforting, and worth the money now if it keeps you out of court later. Ask your attorney the best way to handle all of the following steps.

» **INVESTIGATE QUICKLY AND THOROUGHLY.** Any delays on your part could look bad should an ugly situation get uglier. Besides, it's the right thing to do for the accused and the accuser.

» **HANDLE MISCONDUCT RIGHT AWAY.** That could involve everything from verbal and written warnings to counseling to job transfers to suspension to termination.

» **PROTECT THE RIGHTS OF THE ACCUSED.** Ask your attorney what you can and cannot do.

» **DOCUMENT EVERYTHING.** Accusation, investigation, findings and remedial job actions, if necessary, should be spelled out in writing.

» **FOLLOW UP.** Talk to everyone involved. Is the accuser protected from continued harassment and retribution? Is the accused taking the actions you've requested? Are there other disciplinary steps that need to be taken? Be sure to put all that in writing as well.

Part 3 HEALTH

CHAPTER 45
SELF-ESTEEM AND HEALTH

We all know that self-esteem helps us feel good about ourselves and our abilities. Did you know that self-esteem is important to your health as well?

Researchers have learned that healthy self-esteem – the positive and generally optimistic regard we have for ourselves and our capabilities – is directly connected to how well we handle stress. And stress can have some pretty dire physical complications if left unaddressed.

Some of those conditions include exhaustion, depression, sleep disorders, low energy levels, headaches, chest pains, and frequent colds and infections. Stress can damage the neuroendocrine system that that regulates many body processes, including digestion, moods, emotion and even sexuality.

The higher your **self-esteem** the easier it is to **handle stress**

Empowering Women | Key-Dynamics.com

People who think well of themselves generally have less stress in their lives – not because their lives are perfect and carefree, but because they find it easier to rise to challenges.

It's a perceptual thing.

When something unanticipated comes up – good or bad – they tend to see these events as wonderful opportunities. Because they think well of themselves and their abilities, they know they have what it takes to create a positive outcome.

They anticipate success instead of failure and are much less likely to get stressed over whatever situation causes it.

People with low self-esteem, on the other hand, see the identical challenges as insurmountable burdens. They feel "less than," incapable of handling them and generally incompetent. They have convinced themselves that they are doomed to failure. They believe they do not have what it takes and feel helpless, powerless and overwhelmed.

Yeah. That would stress me out, too.

One of the best ways to boost your self-confidence and your self-esteem is to take a strengths inventory (see workbook), because you truly are better, smarter and stronger than you think.

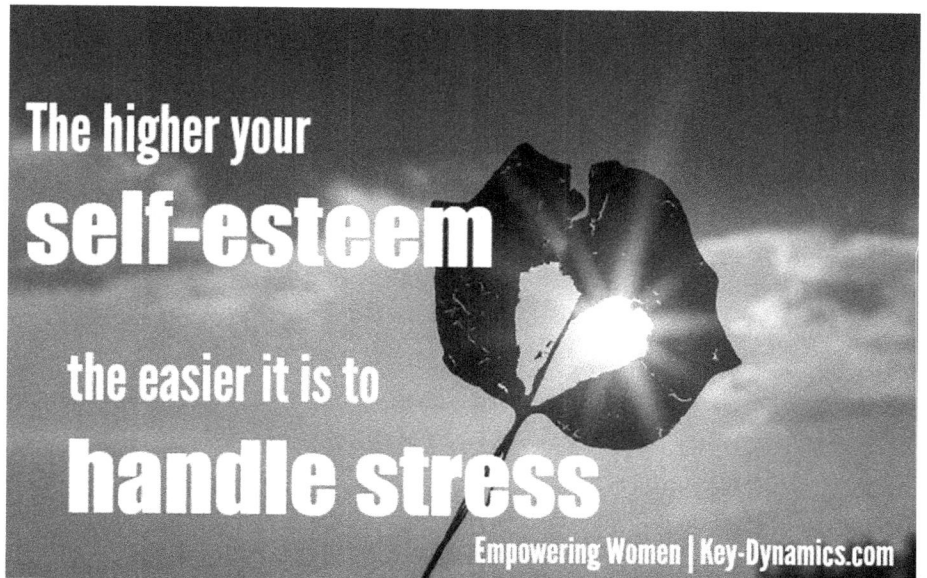

Also, when you get into stressful situations, pay close attention to what you're saying to yourself. Ask, "Is this true or just a story I'm telling myself?"

Another key element to having good self-esteem, and less stress, is to have great assertiveness skills. People with low self-esteem tend to get dumped on by friends, work colleagues and family members because they don't know how to say "No."

When you stand up for yourself, your stress level goes down and your self-esteem and your physical and mental health improve. What's not to like?

Assertiveness skills are not astrophysics. Anyone can learn them and, with practice, they will become second nature.

Even people with good self-esteem can succumb to consistently high levels of stress over long periods, so it's good to have in your toolbox some ways to combat stress. Here are a few.

COACHING REQUEST

>> *IMPROVE YOUR TIME MANAGEMENT*

>> *PRACTICE DEEP BREATHING*

>> *TAKE A 1-MINUTE VACATION – IN YOUR HEAD*

>> *HAVE A SOCIAL SUPPORT SYSTEM IN PLACE.* This is a network of people who appreciate us, flaws and all, and help meet our needs. A 1989 study of women with breast cancer showed that those who had a support network not only had fewer stressors, but lived, on average, 18 months longer compared to the control group.

>> *GIVE SUPPORT TO OTHERS.* A 2003 study showed that people 65 and older who gave support to others lived longer than people who did not.

CHAPTER 46
LISTEN TO YOUR BODY

Are you sick and tired... of being sick and tired? If you are, then chances are excellent you're primed to move on to the Next Big Thing in your life.

Even if you don't realize it.

We are wholly integrated human beings and every part of us affects every other part. Illness, fatigues, aches and pains, depression and even injuries can be symptoms of something else that's bothering us on an emotional or spiritual level. And worry, grief, anger, fear and an entire host of other emotional conditions can physically manifest themselves in our bodies.

The body is literal and if we're paying attention, we can learn things about ourselves that we've hidden in our subconscious.

That killer headache you have could be an indication something is weighing on your mind.

Neck bothering you? Who or what in your life is a pain in the neck? What are you being stubborn and stiff-necked about?

Your upset stomach could be something you ate... or it could be your gut is telling you that you're just sick about something going on in your life.

Back problems can be associated with feeling a lack of support. Stubbing your toe or otherwise hurting your feet may mean you're struggling with moving forward. Slumped shoulders could indicate a feeling of helplessness, hopelessness or carrying a heavy burden.

Injuries or "accidents" – especially those that happen over and over again, to the same part of our bodies – are our inner self's attempt to get our attention. Don't ignore them!

You may think all this is a load of hooey, that people are just clumsy or get sick because someone coughs germs on them or they have a genetic predisposition to some condition. Sometimes it is.

But what if it's not?

Once you're sick and tired of being sick and tired, it's time to explore all the possibilities. Start with this exercise adapted from the Freeze-Frame technique found in *The HeartMath Solution* by Doc Childre and Howard Martin. It's also a great exercise to use when you're looking for the answer to any thorny problem.

COACHING REQUEST

» **FIND A COMFORTABLE SPOT.** Get away from any kind of intrusion. Give yourself about a half hour.

» **THINK BACK.** Cast your mind to a place and time when you were happy, relaxed, loved, stress-free and so on.

» **RE-EXPERIENCE IT.** Put yourself there again, with all your senses – smell, touch, hearing, sight and taste.

» **ASK YOUR HEART.** "What is causing me to feel this way?"

» **LISTEN TO YOUR HEART.** Important note: The answer will be the first thing that comes to you. The second thing that comes up will be your head, which will tell you that you're being irrational, this can't possibly be true, that you're missing other vital information and so on. That is your brain's job – but that doesn't mean it's necessarily correct. Your heart, your intuition, is a shortcut to all your wisdom, life experience and education. Listen to it!

» **TAKE ACTION.** I'm a knowledge junkie, but all the knowledge in the world won't do a damn bit of good if you don't act on it.

CHAPTER 47
HOW TO STOP WORRYING

If you're like many people these days, you're worried... about something.

Why? Worrying never changes the outcome.

There's only one thing worry is good for – and that's motivating you to take action.

Back in my newspaper days, I worried about an abundance of things – what I'd written, what I'd missed – and suffered many sleepless nights as a result.

I remember very clearly my "a-ha" moment, which came late one night as I thrashed around in bed, trying to flip off my worry switch so I could sleep.

It dawned on me, in mid-thrash, that the newspaper had already been printed. What could I possibly do about my worries at that point?

What was worse, the next day I learned that I hadn't made that mistake at all.

Worry falls into two general categories: things that may happen and things that have happened. The key to dealing with both is action. "Doing" is always better than "not doing" when it comes to banishing worry.

Worrying makes you miserable twice – now, about things that may never occur, and in the future, should the worst actually come true.

If the source of your anxiety is in the past, ask yourself, "Is there anything I can do about it now?" If you regret harsh words or actions, would an apology help? Don't forget that you can apologize even to people who are no longer alive.

If you did a lousy job at something, can you fix it or do it again? Can you offer restitution? If the injured person is no longer around, how can you "pay it forward"?

After soul searching, you may discover there is no way you can undo the source of your regret. If there is no action you can take, accept it, sincerely promise yourself you'll do better – and move on with your life.

Sounds easy. It's not. It took me more than 20 years of worrying (with its attendant consequences) before my "a-ha" moment came.

Like any other skill, it takes practice. Start now to put your worry behind you, and learn to enjoy what you have right now.

COACHING REQUEST

» **JOT DOWN YOUR WORRIES AS THEY ARISE.** Don't deal with them at that moment, because the next thing I recommend is to...

» **CREATE WORRY PERIOD.** Set aside 20-30 minutes to just sit and think about what's troubling you. Mid-afternoon would be good; you don't want it so late in the day that it bumps up against bedtime. When your worry period rolls around, review the notes you've made during the day. Then ask:

  ○ **IS THIS REAL OR IMAGINED?** Is this something that's happening in my life right now (like a medical crisis) or is it something I think may happen in the future (such as being too poor to retire)?

  ○ **WHAT ARE THE CHANCES?** If it's a future worry, what is the likelihood it will really happen? Review the facts. Put a percentage on how likely your future worry will come true. If it's less than 50%, decide if it's worth worrying about.

  ○ **TAKE ACTION.** Can I do something about it? If the answer is yes: What steps do I need to take? Action is the antidote to worry.

If worrying keeps you awake at night, see the workbook for tips on how to fall asleep at night.

CHAPTER 48
DEALING WITH OVERWHELM

It's easy for us women to get overwhelmed because we are trying to do so many things at once. We're pulled in so many directions that it's hard to get anything done, let alone get it done right.

We feel buffeted by events and forces not of our making. It feels like the world is going to crash and burn on our heads.

Whatever is overwhelming you, know that you can help take back your life by doing just one thing. It doesn't have to be big or important.

Just do one thing.

COACHING REQUEST

» **STOP SAYING YOU'RE OVERWHELMED.** Remember, you get what you focus on.
» **MONEY – SPENDING LESS.** What one thing can you do to cut back on your expenses? Is it buying house brands instead of name brands? Maybe it's having only one cup of Starbucks a week instead of three, or borrowing a book from the library instead of buying a paperback.
» **MONEY – MAKING MORE.** What one thing can you do to make more money? If the answer is a new or better job, check out employment opportunities. Pull up that old resume and revise it. Sell items in good condition that you no longer use or need.
» **ENVIRONMENT.** What one thing can you do to bring order to chaos? Clean out the junk drawer? File papers? Keep only the stuff you need or is really worth keeping. Someone, somewhere, is worse off than you are and would be grateful for the things you've been hoarding "just in case."

CHAPTER 49
WHAT TO DO WHEN LIFE BEATS YOU DOWN

What do you do when life unexpectedly lands a roundhouse kick to the shins? Most immediate reactions, while gratifying – like striking back, screaming or taking it out on a relatively blameless third party – will only provide short-term relief, if that. And a thoughtless reaction can make matters worse.

Here are a few alternatives:

» **DO NOTHING.** This is almost as destructive as blowing up, especially if what's happened to you is painful. Internalizing bad feelings is a sure way to wear a hole in your stomach. It is not recommended.

» **GET YOUR MAD ON.** Get it out of your system in ways that don't harm you, the people around you, small animals or expensive objects.

» **FIND A CONFIDANT.** Who will give you straight answers instead of telling you what they think you want to hear? But be very careful – if you're dealing with a workplace issue, think twice – and then think again – before you confide in a colleague. If that person isn't as trustworthy as you believe, you could be in a whole new world of hurt.

One you get past the initial shock and hurt, take a step back and figure out constructive ways to deal with it.

COACHING REQUEST

» **WHAT CAUSED THE SITUATION?** What's really going on? Be as objective as you can. Was it something you said or did? Was someone angry about something else and took it out on you? Remember that while something you said or did could have triggered someone's bad behavior, ultimately it is on them. There is something going on in their life that has nothing to do with you.

» **WHAT CAN YOU DO ABOUT IT?**
  ○ If you were wrong, say so. Apologize, promise not to do it ever again and move on.
  ○ If you were a convenient target for someone to vent their ire, you can say that you're sorry they're upset. Be sincere.
  ○ If you were right and you still got kicked in the shins, move to the next level: What do you want? What's the outcome you're trying to achieve? What are you willing to do – and how far are you willing to go – to get there?
  ○ Is it within your power to influence? Can you remedy the situation?

» **WHAT CAN YOU LEARN FROM WHAT'S HAPPENED TO YOU?** You may need to re-evaluate who you consider trustworthy, who is really your friend. You may have to learn how to speak your truth in a different way, or even just think before you speak. You may need to do more research before you commit to a plan of action.

» **WHAT COULD YOU HAVE DONE DIFFERENTLY?** Should you have spoken up or, conversely, kept your head down? Should you have done more due diligence?

CHAPTER 50
MANAGING NEGATIVE EMOTIONS

How do you handle negative feelings?

If your plan is to ignore them until they go away, it's a bad idea. Because they won't. All they do is sit in your subconscious and rot until either they explode on whoever happens to be around – another bad idea — or they take it out on your body.

SOME OF THOSE HEALTH CONSEQUENCES INCLUDE:

» Greater incidence of asthma
» Higher blood pressure
» Lower resistance to infectious disease
» Increased allergic reactions
» Abuse of alcohol or drugs or both
» Overeating and weight gain
» Higher cholesterol levels
» Systemic inflammation, which is connected to heart disease, cancer and Alzheimer's
» Acceleration of aging (just what we need, yes?)
» Other physical reactions include headaches, stomach and digestive issues such as ulcers, fatigue, depression, low back pain, neck pain and arthritis. Sudden emotional shocks can even cause heart attacks in healthy people. Notably, most of those were women.

In fact, the Centers for Disease Control and Prevention estimate that 90% of doctors' visits are linked to stress and the negative feelings that stress engenders.

When it comes to emotions, it's "damned if you do, damned if you don't."

The very thing that can make women sick is also what makes them so great in business. Because they have high levels of emotional intelligence – or EQ – they can pick up on the feelings of others, manage people better and help build respect, trust and rapport.

It gives them a collaborative approach to business dealings, instead of the traditional "my way or the highway," top-down method of management. Their EQ also allows them to look at situations as "us vs. the problem" as opposed to "us vs. them."

Not only that, but their EQ gives them powerful motivation because they can more easily connect their goals to the feelings they will have when they reach them.

These same emotions have taken many a woman to the brink of tears (or over the edge) in stressful personal and professional situations due to stress or sheer, towering rage.

No woman wants that. So they decide, somewhere along the way, that the only way they can be successful is by suppressing their feelings. Many of us have gotten so good at stuffing them is that we have become hard – and hard to get along with. Otherwise known as "bitchy."

How do you make your emotions work for you instead of against you? Is it even possible? Yes. Check out the following Coaching Request for the deets.

COACHING REQUEST

>> ***IDENTIFY WHAT YOU'RE FEELING.*** Many women have done such a great job of pushing down every negative emotion that they aren't really sure what they're feeling anymore. A few ideas: Unhappy, pissed off, annoyed, vengeful, abused, anxious, cruel, defeated, broken down, envious, disgusted and so on. Don't judge your emotions (something that we're really good at!); just identify.

>> ***FEEL IT***. I don't care that you don't want to feel that way. You do, and ignoring that doesn't make it go away. The sooner you let yourself experience them, the better off you will be. And the sooner they will disappear.

>> ***SAY IT OUT LOUD.*** In front of a mirror is even better: "I am angry. I am dissatisfied. I am sad. I am confused. I am paranoid." Whatever you're feeling, give voice to it. If you need to scream, shout, throw things, pound on tables – go ahead. Get it out of your system. (Note to readers who are still in their child-bearing years or going through menopause – it gets easier once you're not held hostage by your hormones. When you are in the throes of a hormonal meltdown, understand that it, too, shall pass. That will relieve some of the negative feelings you're experiencing. And if 25% of your life is totally out of control due to your menstrual cycle, please see your doc. Something ain't right.)

>> ***RELEASE IT.*** Once you've purged, go back to your mirror and say to yourself, out loud: "I release envy from my life. I release anger. I release shame." Whatever you need to let go of, say it out loud. Someone is listening: You. I did that with an ex-husband who, 18 years after our split, still regularly haunted my dreams. It worked like a charm for me - no more dreams.

>> ***REPLACE IT.*** Negative feelings are toxic – to your body, heart, mind and soul. The sooner you can focus on positive feelings, the better off you will be. Count your blessings: "I am strong. I am worthy. I am smart. I am responsible." If the best you can do is state, "I woke up this morning," that's a good start.

If you're at work and someone has hurt your feelings and you want to either to kick someone's butt or sob your eyes out, take the following steps.

>> ***FOCUS ON YOUR INTAKE AND OUTFLOW OF BREATH.*** Count each one. Notice how it expands and deflates your ribcage. Imagine pure, cleansing oxygen reaching every part of your body and how each exhale releases toxins. See how deep breathing helps regulate your heart rate and soothes your nerves.

>> ***ALTERNATIVE 1: KEEP QUIET.*** If you feel that anything that might come out of your mouth would be damning or tear-stained blubbering, stay silent or use filler words like "uh-huh," "I see" and so on. That way the other person knows you're not sleeping with your eyes open. Whatever you do, don't nod. Men see nodding as agreement and if you're getting your ass handed to you for no good reason, the last thing you want to do is look like you're agreeing.

>> **ALTERNATIVE 2: ASK QUESTIONS.** This depends on the situation, but you might ask something like, "How did you arrive at that conclusion? What makes you think that way? What do you think the solution is? How do you think we should move forward? What did I do wrong and how can I fix it?" By asking for objective data and clear feedback, you'll take the focus – yours and his – off how you feel.

>> **AVOID "WHY" QUESTIONS.** Even in the most neutral circumstances, questions that start with "why" can sound like accusations. Maybe they deserve to be, but that's not helpful. You want to keep a handle on your emotions, not throw gas on the embers.

>> **GO TO YOUR HAPPY PLACE.** Your boss (or client) is chewing you up one side and down another, justified or not. There isn't a single thing you can do about it until it's over, at which time you can do the scream-shout-pound-on-tables thing mentioned earlier. Until then, imagine yourself in your favorite place, surrounded by your favorite people/things, eating your favorite foods and let him rant.

>> **FINALLY, UNDERSTAND THAT YOU ARE IN CHARGE OF YOU.** If the other person is a bully, there is nothing he would like better than to get a rise out of you. Don't give him the satisfaction! Often that internalized "I'll show you!" attitude can prevent an emotional outburst.

CHAPTER 51
WHY YOU GET BETTER AS YOU GET OLDER

With age comes experience. And, if you're lucky, a wee bit of wisdom, too.

Here are just a few reasons why women get better as we get older.

> "The only source of **knowledge** is **experience**."
> ~ Albert Einstein

>> You're less inclined to put up with people's crap.

>> You saw the great bands before they became famous.

>> You get a senior's discount (but it's better to ask for it than to have others assume you're an old fart).

>> You can start collecting Social Security and, if you're lucky enough to have one, a pension, too.

>> Your dearest, most treasured friends tell you how amazingly young you look and ask for your secret.

>> You realize that if people have a problem with you, that's exactly what it is – their problem. Not yours.

>> You don't give a fig what most other people think about you.

>> You're likely to scandalize your younger relatives by what you say or do because...hey. What the hell. Why not?

>> You have a first-person perspective on what younger people call "history." If they even know what that is.

>> You know it's not the end of the world. Whatever it is. This, too, shall pass.

>> Just when you think you've seen it all, something else happens. Life is still a surprise and worth treasuring.

>> You do less stupid stuff, because you did most of it before.

>> You are still hot – it just comes in flashes.

>> You look back at your 20s and say, "Thank God THAT'S over!"

>> You recognize how smart your parents were.

>> You woke up. Yay! Any day above the dirt is a good day.

>> There are just some things that are not worth getting worked up about. Make that "most things."

>> You owned classic cars before they were classics. And wish you still had them now. (My 1965 Mustang fastback is the only car I sold for more money than I paid for it.)

>> You've gotten really good at spotting manipulators.

>> You can more easily release the things – and people – that no longer serve you.

>> You have learned the hard way that you never loan money to relatives. Call it a gift and let it go.

>> You have a much clearer vision of what's important in your life.

>> Your definition of success has migrated from the outer trappings of life to what makes you happy.

>> You refuse to get sucked into other people's drama.

>> You matter to yourself – you've moved up on your own list of important people in your life.

» You realize you're not perfect and you never will be. You're OK with that. It's the imperfections that make you unique...and memorable (hopefully in a good way. But if not – hey, what the hell).

» You're better at recognizing your own value and that you know a lot of stuff. More than you thought you did.

» You've given up trying to change other people because you know (a) it's not your business and (b) it's hard enough to change yourself.

» You understand that some people are always going to be negative and whiny and the sooner you bounce them from your life, the better off you'll be.

» You FINALLY understand that worry will never change the outcome, that it only steals your present joy.

» You're more comfortable in your own (sagging and wrinkled) skin.

» You've learned that even well-intentioned advice is not welcome, so you keep it to yourself unless you're asked.

» When you wake up in the morning, you recognize that it's totally in your power to have a good day or a bad day.

» And speaking of bad days: You've survived 100% of the worst days of your life. *Celebrate!*

CHAPTER 52
THE YEAR IN REVIEW

You've done tons of work in the last year. Great job! It wasn't easy, but you are well on your way to being where you want to be.

Here are some questions to ask yourself as you move forward.

COACHING REQUEST

Make a list.

>> How are you better off today than you were a year ago?

>> How often to you schedule "me" time?

>> How has your thinking about yourself changed?

>> What are you doing differently today?

>> What have you learned from your mistakes?

>> What's the biggest change you've made in your life?

>> What are you doing to sustain yourself?

>> How do you handle people who drain your energy?

>> What do you want?

>> What is your plan to get to where you want to be?

>> Are you on track?

>> Are you living your life with intention?

>> What healthful ways have you adopted to deal with stress?

>> What are you focusing on?

>> What is your body telling you – right this minute?

>> Who do you need to forgive so you can move forward?

>> How has your perspective shifted?

>> What are you doing to grow yourself, personally and professionally?

>> If you could get rid of one thing in your life right now, what would it be?

>> What's one change you want to make in your life, right now?

>> What's next for you?

Congratulations!

You made it!

How do you feel? Empowered? Strong? Smart? Determined? That sound you hear is my standing ovation for you!

If you feel just as overwhelmed as when you started reading, cheer up, my darling. No one makes major life changes overnight.

You'll have missteps. You'll backslide. You'll beat yourself up again. You'll be distracted by bright, shiny objects. You'll let people take advantage of you.

That's OK. You're human, which means "imperfect."

But you'll also discover that you're not as wishy-washy as you used to be. You do speak up and take credit more often than before. You are taking better care of yourself. Just keep going! No one gets it right the first time, or every time. Cut yourself some slack, for crying out loud! As with any new skill, you'll get better at it the more you do it. Plus, you now have the knowledge and the tools to help you get back on track.

Finally, if sections of this book just pissed you off: Yay! Always, always pay attention to any information or idea that provokes a strong emotional reaction. Revisit those parts and ask why you got angry or thought it was ridiculous or stupid or any of those other feelings. I'll bet you a café mocha that's the first place you should focus.

Thanks for being with me. I hope you got tons of information from this book and that it propels you further than you ever dreamed possible!

I would love to hear your comments and your success stories.

Feel free to drop me a line: jackie@key-dynamics.com. If you're interested in a complementary coaching session, let's set it up.

To your success!

Jackie

Index

A

Accomplishments 49
Adult Children 43
Advocate 43
Aggressive 59
Aging 93
Alphabet Game 26
Assertiveness
   Broken Record
      Negative Assertion 39

B

Balance 71
   Work-Life 71
Behavior 22, 23, 35, 76
Beliefs 11, 59, 71
Boss, Being The 54, 70, 74, 84

C

Career 5, 28, 76
Caretakers 36
Challenges 7, 12, 60, 86
Change 21, 27, 30, 32, 41
Changing 20
Coaching 2, 4, 14, 29, 36
Communication 62, 68
Control Freak 76
Criticism 46
   Criticized 12
   Criticizes 46

D

Delegation 53
   Delegate 67

E

Emotional Intelligence 93
   Eq 93
Emotions 93, 94
Empower 26
   Empowered 23
Energy 13, 15, 41, 42, 86
Entitlement 43
Entrepreneurs 72

F

Failure 8, 9, 24, 64, 86
Faith 28, 59
Fear 64
   Of Failure 64
   Of Success 64

Feedback 62
   Feedback File 60
Feelings 69, 74, 75
   Bad Feelings 92
   Emotions 93
      Expressing 69
      Managing 93
      Negative Emotions 93
Financial 49, 50
Flex Space 71
Flex Time 71

G

Goals 20
   Setting 19
   SMART 65
Gossip 68
Gratitude 31, 33
Guilt 2, 21, 22, 27, 31
   Guilty 69

H

Handshake 78, 80
Harvard Business School 19, 49
Health 71, 77, 86, 93
   Mental 71
   Physical 71
   Spiritual 71
Heartmath Solution 12, 88
   Freeze-Frame 12, 88
Household Chores 72
   Housework 5, 72

I

Ideal Job 48
Imposter Syndrome 60
Inside Time 55
Interruptions 54
Investments 10
I Statement 23, 43

J

Job Sharing 71
Judgment 18, 22, 34, 44, 46, 82

L

Law of Attraction 41, 42, 62
Leadership 49, 58, 60
Learning 8, 29, 36, 41
Lies 25
Life Purpose 15, 29
Listening 58, 94

M

Maltz, Dr. Maxwell 62
   Psycho-Cybernetics 62
   Success Mechanism 62
Management 26, 49, 52, 54, 60,
      65, 87, 93
Meetings 56, 57, 68
Mentoring 44
Micromanage 54
Mindset 11, 12, 50
   Abundance 42, 89
   Scarcity 42
Mirror Work 26
Mommy Penalty 49
Money 2, 17, 56, 73, 84, 91
Motivation 4
   External 30
   Internal 30
Motivation 30
Multitasking 66

N

Negotiations 50, 51
   Negotiating 49, 51
Networking 78, 80, 82

O

Obstacles 12
   Clearing 12
Opinions 44
   Other People's 44
Opportunities 8, 20, 27, 53, 66, 86
Outsource 73
Overwhelm 24, 51, 67, 91

P

Passion 4, 17, 46, 58
Passive-Aggressive 69
Perfectionist 76
   Perfectionism 67
Performance 53, 56, 76
   Job 55, 77
Personal Power 9, 40
Phony 61
Praise 53, 77
Priorities 52
Problem 22, 60, 77
   Solving 77
Procrastination 66, 67
Progressive Discipline 53
Public Speaking 82
   Public Speaker 25
Pushback 23, 43

R

Reframe 12, 46
   Thinking 24
Reinvent Yourself 13
Relationship 13, 34, 40, 71, 74
Retirement 10, 49
Risk 8, 37, 40, 64
   Low-Risk 40

S

Self-Esteem 9, 34, 86, 87
Self-Love 50
Self-Talk 9, 48, 67
Self-Worth 45, 60
Sexual Harassment 84
Sexuality 86
Stay-At-Home Mom 72
Strengths 4, 29, 46
Stress 32, 59, 71, 76
Success 7, 62, 86, 96
   Success File 60
Support 87
   Support Systems 87

T

Taking Action 27
Taking Advantage 11, 39
Team 52, 53
Technology 71
Therapy 2
Time Management 26, 52, 65, 87
Toxic People 34, 35
Training 10, 44, 48, 55

V

Vision 15, 49, 96

W

Weasel Words 51
   What Not To Say 51
Worry 20, 45, 89
   Worry Period 89
Worth 10, 19, 84
   Monetary 35

www.ingramcontent.com/pod-product-compliance
Lightning Source LLC
Chambersburg PA
CBHW081226040426

42445CB00016B/1904